F

THE 800-COCAINE BOOK OF DRUG AND ALCOHOL RECOVERY

JAMES COCORES, M.D.

A FIRESIDE BOOK
PUBLISHED BY SIMON & SCHUSTER
NEW YORK   LONDON   TORONTO   SYDNEY   TOKYO   SINGAPORE

FIRESIDE
Simon & Schuster Building
Rockefeller Center
1230 Avenue of the Americas
New York, New York 10020

First Fireside Edition 1991
Published by arrangement with Villard Books, a division of Random
House, Inc.

FIRESIDE and colophon are registered trademarks of Simon & Schuster
Inc.

Manufactured in the United States of America

10 9 8 7 6 5 4 3 2 1

Library of Congress Cataloging in Publication Data
Cocores, James.
    The 800-cocaine book of drug and alcohol recovery/James Cocores.—
1st Fireside ed.
        p.   cm.
    "A Fireside book."
    Reprint. Originally published: New York: Villard Books, 1990.
    Includes bibliographical references and index.
        1. Alcoholics—Rehabilitation.   2. Narcotic addicts—
Rehabilitation.   3. Substance abuse—Popular works.   I. Title.
    [RC565.C517   1991]
    362.29—dc20   91-20094
                                                                  CIP
ISBN 0-671-74486-0

Grateful acknowledgment is made to *People Weekly* for permission to reprint
an excerpt from "A Veteran TV Anchorman's Toughest Story Was His
Own—He Had to Beat Drugs and Depression" by Jim Jensen, September 4,
1989 issue.

To my parents Helen and Steve
To my dearest companion and love, Mary,
and our daughters, Eleni and Alexandra

FOREWORD BY
MARK S. GOLD, M.D.

TODAY, MOST PEOPLE KNOW THAT DRUGS, ESPECIALLY CO-
caine, are dangerous and often fatal. It's hard to believe that less
than a decade ago most people thought that substance abuse
could be purely recreational and even glamorous. Fortunately,
because of what we have learned from a wide range of sources—
including the essential research provided by the national help-
line, 800-COCAINE—all of us now recognize how damaging
and dangerous drugs like cocaine and crack really are. Over
three million callers to the 800-COCAINE hotline pinpointed
the need for a new form of treatment, called Outpatient Recovery Centers (ORC). These centers provide the latest medical
information, emphasize the importance of education in recovery, and bring successful treatments to the person's neighborhood.

Medicine in general, and psychiatry in particular, have largely
ignored the problems of substance abuse and addiction. It's been
only through the efforts of hundreds of thousands of recovering
addicts in Alcoholics Anonymous (AA) that modern medicine
and psychiatry has responded to the seriousness of the problem.

When we began 800-COCAINE, most people using drugs were not treated. Even self-help groups like AA and Narcotics Anonymous (NA) were not given a chance by the cocaine user. The challenge was to use twelve-step programs like AA in a manner that worked for the cocaine user. These programs have always been—and still remain—at the root of recovery for anyone with a drug or alcohol problem.

As addiction and drug use rose in the late 1970s and early 1980s, the basic response from the medical community was exclusively to provide inpatient programs for those who could not succeed in a twelve-step program. In fact, Fair Oaks was in the forefront of treatment for cocaine addiction, establishing the nation's first inpatient cocaine treatment programs in 1978. It was slowly imitated by hundreds of others. While successful, these inpatient programs were limited by availability, expense, and qualified treatment specialists. The overwhelming response to the 800-COCAINE hotline clearly indicated that the majority of cocaine addicts were not receiving treatment. Even those who were being treated were typically receiving less than optimal treatment. One reason we began 800-COCAINE was to learn even more about the effects of this drug on people who were not in treatment. But 800-COCAINE has had a dual effect: We learned from people in a "living laboratory" just how damaging these and other drugs were; in turn, people found a resource to get help quickly.

As more people learned about 800-COCAINE they began to call for information about a loved one's problem, for help, and for treatment referrals. From their calls we recognized a need for a different type of recovery program. Many were lucky enough to call before they had lost their jobs, families, and even their lives.

From this need we created a new type of program that combined the twelve-step traditions of AA with intensive treatment techniques in a setting that could be tailored to an individual's needs. In 1985 we began to explore ways that substance abusers could be treated in an outpatient program as effectively as in an inpatient. The Outpatient Recovery Centers of Fair Oaks Hospital enables those addicted to receive treatment in a cost effective setting. In addition, they can remain at their jobs, continue to live and function at home, go to school, and lead a relatively normal life while still receiving the benefits of an intensive therapeutic program.

Today, ORC is the single largest provider of substance abuse recovery services in New Jersey. Over ten thousand adults and adolescents have been successfully treated at our five locations. From these patients, we have learned the importance of a broad-based, lifelong approach to recovery.

Dr. James Cocores, who has been medical director of ORC since its opening, has guided the creative and effective development of the ORC recovery strategies. The constantly evolving programs incorporate the best aspects of the twelve-step model with the latest medical information about the effects of drugs and the importance of nutrition, exercise, therapy, and medication in treatment and recovery and include an early intervention program for adolescents, school programs for teenage patients, a partial hospitalization (The Day Hospital) program, evening and weekend programs to enable patients to maintain their job status, and programs designed for adult children of alcoholics.

In addition, ORC has become a vital resource for the community at large, putting on hundreds of educational programs for lay and professional audiences. We have learned that education leads to prevention—and that's the best treatment we have.

ACKNOWLEDGMENTS

I AM GRATEFUL TO MARK S. GOLD, M.D., FOUNDER OF 800-COCAINE, who fostered this book.

I wish to acknowledge the contributions of Charles Dackis, M.D., Robert Stuckey, M.D., Joseph Harrison, Art Prinz, Dorothy Brocar, Melinda Farnsworth, Fern Steinberg, Joan Dixon, Richard Jensen, Barbara Kent, Michael Newman, Ginny Robichaud, Kurt Scheckermann, Roni Lonoff, Denise Stoklosa, and my patients. Each person helped me understand and organize my thinking about recovery.

Special thanks for their professional and editorial assistance to Mae Rudolph and Dan Montopoli.

Finally, I am very grateful to Villard Books, especially the outstanding efforts of my editor, Alison Acker, Peter Gethers, and Janis Donnaud.

CONTENTS

1
WHAT IS RECOVERY?

"And the secret of happiness," mocked Tastevin, "is to refrain from smoking?"

"The secret of happiness," Datt corrected, "is to refrain from *wishing to.*"

—from *An Expensive Place to Die* by Len Deighton

AT THE BEGINNING OF RECOVERY YOU MAY NOT BE SURE JUST what it is you want or expect. You may know only that you can't stand it anymore the way it has been. You may have been so far down that you had reached the point where all you knew was that you didn't want to die. You may think that what you want is what almost every chemically dependent person seems to want at first—to be able to use drink or drugs "like normal people," that is, with all the "fun" but without the horrible consequences they have had for you. You may expect that once you've become abstinent for any length of time at all, you'll be "cured"; that just stopping will make it possible to stop forever, without any trouble.

Or perhaps you've quit already—and fallen off the wagon, unable to sustain the discipline, not getting the support it takes to stay clean and sober. Maybe you think living sober is for other people, people who are tough enough to hack it. Maybe you never understood what recovery would mean in the first place. Going it alone and going cold turkey doesn't work for most people, but how could you know if you've placed yourself in virtual solitary confinement with your addiction?

That's where this book comes in. Five years ago Mark S. Gold, M.D. at Fair Oaks Hospital published a revolutionary book called *800-COCAINE*. It contained information about cocaine addiction, and at the time that was big news. Everyone thought cocaine was just another stop along the way to a good time. The "glamour" drug—that's what people were calling cocaine. No one took the "glamour" drug seriously until people started dying. Star athletes like Len Bias were dropping dead, and it was all because of cocaine. Now our headlines are filled daily with stories about drugs and the war on drugs. Now people are deadly serious about cocaine, but some of them are already hooked.

The 800-COCAINE Book of Drug and Alcohol Recovery picks up where *800-COCAINE* left off. It will guide you through recovery from start to finish, starting with abstinence and ending with true recovery—a new life that will really be worth living. And it will teach you the difference between abstinence—just quitting—and recovery, and why recovery makes so much real sense.

The truth is, abstinence—giving up alcohol or drugs entirely—is not recovery, although it's the absolutely necessary first step. Abstinence *alone* should never be the final goal. A lifetime of recovery tormented by constant urges for a line of coke or a joint or that after-work cocktail—what the experts call "white-knuckle sobriety"—will almost always fail. It's like gritting your teeth and just barely hanging on. It's nothing like as bad as being an alcoholic or drug abuser, but it's not great. Real recovery *is* great.

The ideal—and it is achievable—is to reach that point of personal development and integration that could be compared to what athletes call "finding the zone." The zone is a state in which some athletes suddenly feel that their performance is inspired and effortless, as if they were not concentrating on their

actions at all but the actions performed themselves—and at a
higher level than they had ever before achieved.

The zone is that point where one has mastered the skills or
techniques (in your case, the techniques of abstinence, of good
problem solving—of daily living without drugs—where the
techniques have become a part of you; not something you do
but something you *are*. You no longer have to think about
staying sober, you just are. The zone is where something in-
definable within yourself takes over the conscious effort, bring-
ing mastery with it. The great Brazilian soccer player Pelé has
described the athlete's version of the zone like this:

> It was a type of euphoria; I felt I could run all day without
> tiring, that I could dribble through any of their team or
> all of them, that I could pass through them physically. I
> felt I could not be hurt. It was a very strange feeling and
> one I had not felt before. Perhaps it was merely confidence,
> but I have felt confident many times before without the
> strange feeling of invincibility.

This is very close to the way my recovering alcoholic or drug-
abusing patients describe their feelings. The truth is, they actually tell me they are "grateful" for having had their illness,
because without it, they don't believe they ever would have
achieved the personal transformation they have undergone.

This is also the truth: there are millions of people in the world
who have been alcohol or drug dependent, who now live full
and satisfying lives without *wanting drink or drugs*, without for
one moment wishing they could go back to it, without for one
moment feeling sorry for themselves because they're "not like
other people" when it comes to chemicals. This includes a lot
of people who had hit bottom so deep that no one could imagine
they could ever get up.

It can include you.

And this is the truth: it will take time—and work. There will be moments when it may not seem worth it. There will be pain. But there was so much more pain when you were dependent, when even drugs or alcohol didn't seem worth it, either—but at that time there wasn't anything you could see that was better. And if you did glimpse it, you didn't know how to get there.

You will soon see that recovery is not just better, it's *living*. And that's where this book—an outgrowth of our Fair Oaks Outpatient Recovery Center's plan for recovery—comes in. We will help you chart a course to recovery. I can't promise that there won't be rough spots, but I *can* promise that I will share with you the medical knowledge we have about addiction and how it works, and why it happens in the first place. Because it's with understanding that real recovery begins. That, then, is where we'll start.

How This Book Can Help You

Real recovery, as I have said, is not merely abstinence. This concept is difficult for many people, especially those in the early stages of treatment, really to understand. After all, drinking and drug taking were the focal point of their lives before treatment, so it's only natural that they might think of *not* drinking, *not* using cocaine, and *not* lighting up a joint as the definition of recovery. But not using drugs is just abstinence, and although it's a crucial part of recovery it's not enough. I like to tell my patients that:

Abstinence is "I can't," but recovery is "I can."

You *can* live without drinking or drugs, you *can* lead a life filled with personal growth, freedom, and surprisingly powerful pleasures.

Listen to how Gordon, a recovering alcoholic patient of mine, describes recovery:

I'm a sailor. I used to go out to the boat and all I was thinking about was making sure I had enough beer and liquor, loading up the dinghy and stashing it away, checking to make sure there was plenty of ice, thinking about taking that first drink on board. The first thing I would do as soon as we got away from the mooring and the sails were full was to get that drink in my hand. And making sure my friends had plenty, and spending the day in a haze, thinking I was enjoying sailing like I could enjoy nothing else. Drinking and sailing were inseparable. The funny thing is, I thought it was that way for everyone. Lots of people went sailing to party, lots of people brought along some cold beer, so how was I any different?

When I stopped drinking the thing that bothered me most was wondering how on earth I could still go sailing . . . how I could enjoy it without that drink in my hand, especially when everyone was still cracking open a beer?

Now I go out and I can tell you that especially at night, when the stars are crowding the sky and the fluorescence is sparkling in the water and the sails are white in the darkness and the air is so clean you can taste it—there's nothing like that in the world. I can't understand how I could ever have thought that what I was doing before was sailing, when all I was really doing was drinking on a boat.

Several months ago I asked myself how this book could help people like Gordon toward their goal of recovery. It soon became clear that this book must help its readers the way a good treatment program helps its participants. Now, in no way can this book replace a treatment program. Years of directing the Outpatient Recovery Center at Fair Oaks Hospital have proved to me beyond a doubt that there is simply no substitute for the support, guidance, and experience found in a good program. But this book can augment a treatment program and even help guide you to a good one. And in giving you that information I hope to prepare you and help you overcome the often surprising challenges of recovery. I believe strongly that if you're armed with the right information and the right support and guidance from a good treatment program, you can and will lead a sober life.

So, here are the goals of this book, the steps I see along the way to a successful recovery:

First, it will help you recognize the illness and what it implies for your health, your job, your family, your life. I'm a doctor so I usually see the physical—the medical—side of things, and in recovery there are some important facts you should know about how your body responds to the absence of drugs. I'll share that with you along with the wisdom I've gained by working with addicts in recovery. Remember: You may not have the power to change your life without help, but you do have the power to *decide* to change it. This entails breaking down the system of denial that is common to all alcoholics or drug abusers. It does not concern itself in particular with burrowing into the past to find out the whys of your dependence; the past is only important background to what's happening in your life *now* and what you're going to do about it. So getting the facts straight and deciding to change is the first step.

Second, this book will help you admit that you need help, that you can't do it by sheer willpower alone, and it will help guide you to the right kind of treatment center for you. It will help you evaluate whether you should opt for inpatient or out-patient treatment, and it will give you questions to ask when you're investigating various facilities.

Third, it will guide you through the stages of early recovery when your body may be telling you it can't live without drugs but something in your head is telling you *you must or you'll die*. There are real and predictable physical symptoms that come with recovery, especially in the earliest stages of withdrawal. And later there are real, medically treatable side effects, and simply knowing about them you can be prepared to deal with them. Diet, exercise, and what medications you take—along with those you must *not* take—all play a role. I'll give you the best of what my medical background has taught me about them, and then I'll share with you the best, most essential ingredient of all: hope.

Just as there are physical symptoms in recovery there are emotional signposts. The *fourth* goal of this book is to lay out for you the emotional course of recovery, the model for which is the twelve steps of Alcoholics Anonymous (AA). No single organization has done more to fight alcoholism and addiction than AA, and in my opinion any program that ignores what AA has achieved isn't worth your while. Today AA has over two million members worldwide, with approximately one million members in the United States alone. Most people can find a nearby AA meeting—in Manhattan alone there are almost one thousand meetings every week!

Along with these basic elements, a good treatment program provides a *fifth* element: a *nonchemical* substitute for alcohol or drugs that lasts a lifetime. In the recovery world we call this *aftercare*. This means therapy, support, group interaction, a new focus for life, and in general, a nonchemical solution to the problems you may have had before your addiction started. In aftercare you should learn practical and effective ways of solving the problems that contributed to your early use, and help you come to a better understanding of those problems. Often people who have been using chemicals to avoid their problems find that—when sober—their difficulties aren't as bad as they feared. Therapy and group support will help them see why.

MICHAEL

Michael, a recovering alcoholic in his late thirties, provides a good example of how this confusion over the underlying problems can work against a person's successful recovery:

I always felt like an intruder, like I didn't belong here, like if I said or did something wrong everybody would see right through me. Everything had to be just right, the clothes, the talk, that drink in my hand—they were all part of my "pose." I was an account executive for a big advertising agency—I had to kowtow to the client, and I had to do it in style. The clients got whatever they wanted—and what I thought they wanted was a good time. That meant drinking, only the expensive stuff. It was all paid for by my agency, so what did I care?

Well, I started drinking all the time, even when I had to drive. I didn't kill anybody, but I did get a DWI. The judge scared me; one more ticket and she threatened to take away my license for ten years. So I figured I'd cut back. It worked, for a couple of days. But I couldn't stand it, I felt that I was on life sentence. I could see my whole career going down the tube. I had to have that drink in my hand or my clients would walk away from me. So I started drinking again, but only with clients. Hah. You've heard of "social drinkers"? Well, I used to call myself a "career drinker." The joke was on me, though, and boy, did I pay the price. I lost my license and my job at the agency.

Michael did eventually find his way to AA, and it was there that the road to recovery began for him. What he didn't understand before he quit drinking was that his problem was not because of his job—he didn't really need that drink to entertain his clients. Michael's problem was drinking. But even after he'd gotten the booze out of his system there was a lot he had to deal with—and that's where treatment comes in.

Treatment will help you work through what may have helped get your drinking or drug problem started in the first place. Like Michael, most of us want to be in control; no one wants to admit to a problem, much less to a "weakness." But knowing that you are addicted to drugs or alcohol requires that you admit to having a problem—addiction—and the best you can do now is get the help you need.

Before you begin your own recovery, and before I go on to discuss it in more detail, I must address the issue of so-called controlled use. At some point in almost every person's recovery the fantasy crops up that goes something like this: "I'll kick this addiction, stay clean (sober) for a while. Then, when I know what I'm doing, I'll ease back into it, just drink for fun when I *really* want it . . ." The little voice may be sounding in your head even as you read this page. You may be thinking that if you really learn about addiction and how it works that you may be able to drink or use drugs in a controlled way, that as long as you're *smart* about it you'll be able to have fun like everyone else. Think again.

The truth is, "controlled use" is extremely controversial in the field of chemical dependence; at least among the theorists there are actually some people who believe it might be possible. But among most counselors and physicians who deal day-to-day with chemical dependence, there's no real argument. There have been some scientific experiments with controlled use that suggest that certain people can learn to drink or take drugs in a controlled way. Most of the successes have come only through intense and carefully designed training, but the failures *by far* outweigh the successes. The question is, do you really want to place yourself against such impossible odds, when by quitting entirely—and I guarantee this to be true—your life will *definitely* be better? The most widely held belief, and one that I place my bets on, is that the chances of long-term controlled drinking without a lapse back into dependence are so slender that it is not even worth thinking about—that it encourages too easily the denial that is part of this disease called addiction. If you are an addict you are *not* like other people who can drink or use drugs in a controlled way; thinking otherwise just isn't worth the risk.

Just to give you an idea of what's ahead, I want to introduce you to some of the emotional issues that are tied up in a successful recovery. You may have been addicted for a long time or a short time; you may already have hit rock bottom or you may still be on your way down. No two addicts are alike, and no one is promising that your recovery will happen overnight, along a neat, straight line. But there are patterns, and knowing what you can expect will help you move in the right direction, toward health and a better life, free of drugs and alcohol.

The Goals of Recovery: Acceptance

Along with abstinence or even before it the first step is *to accept that you are an alcohol or drug abuser*. This admission brings with it a new identity: you are no longer someone who drinks or takes drugs, you are a person who has made a decision to take hold of your life and turn it around. That in itself is something to be proud of, even if you haven't done much else to be proud of lately. You are now a recovering person, not that other person who was mired in helplessness and hopelessness. But in exchange for using alcohol or drugs to *ward off* depression, guilt, and shame you will now begin learning how to *feel* depression, guilt, shame, and all the other genuine emotions without feeling like a "bad person"—at least that will come in time. For now, when those new feelings first begin to occur, accept them as a gift; they may give you some rough moments, but they are part of the rich new life you've just begun.

Prepare for the "High," but Expect the Worst

In the 1960s, drug use and spirituality—a search for your inner being—often went hand in hand. The antiestablishment message of "drop out, turn on, and tune out" promised spiritual freedom, insights into the mysteries of life. But what it promised and what it really delivered were very different. Most people quickly found out that the answers didn't lie with LSD.

Real recovery can lead to inner spirituality, without the dangers of drugs. Especially early in recovery, many people feel literally *high* from excitement, a sense of adventure, a fresh start of new possibilities. These are good feelings, and you should rejoice in them. They are real, and any recovering person has earned the right to experience them. But after this initial high there is almost always a letdown as you realize that recovery— in and of itself—is no miracle panacea for the problems in your life. If you're not prepared for this drop, it can be devastating. You might feel yourself remembering the good times during your drinking or drug taking with renewed nostalgia. Don't fall for it. Anticipate the initial high, and prepare for the nearly inevitable letdown and the continuing challenges that recovery will pose. There will be lows during recovery, don't get seduced into thinking that you've licked your addiction. But the lows of recovery, as bad as they may seem, aren't anything like the crash from a drug or alcohol high, or the feeling as of being strung out with no place else to go but further down. Recovery can't eliminate every down period—after all these lows are a part of being a human—but it can help you through these times without the disastrous crutch of alcohol or drugs.

The Goals of Recovery:
Realize that Addiction Is a Disease

As you work through recovery you will confront a great many responses and attitudes, ranging from support and compassion to perplexity and even open hostility. Whatever the other people in your life might be saying, what matters most is your own attitude about your addiction and the brave step you are taking by fighting it. The current view of the medical profession, which is supported by recent genetic, clinical, and neuropharmacological research, is that alcoholism and drug addiction are *diseases* of the mind and central nervous system. Alcoholism and drug addiction can be defined as a pattern of behavioral, psychological, and physical symptoms that result from an interaction between alcohol or drugs and the brain. Addiction happens in people with a genetic susceptibility to it but its occurrence is influenced by personal and social factors. That's the long version. The short version is that addiction, like certain kinds of cancer or diabetes, tends to run in families, but having a family member who's an addict doesn't necessarily mean you'll become addicted, too. It also doesn't mean you're to blame if you *do*. Does anyone blame a person who gets diabetes? Certainly not. Blaming someone else—or yourself—for an addiction is just as wrong and just as unproductive. But what if the diabetic refuses to take insulin properly, or insists on a diet high in sugar? Or consider the person with lung cancer who continues to smoke, or the alcoholic who continues to drink. Are these people solely victims of a disease, or should they accept some responsibility? This is one of the most difficult subjects in recovery, and there is no easy answer. I believe that addiction is clearly a disease, but a disease whose treatment requires the person to take responsibility for his or her health. If you are in recovery, you have already begun to take responsibility for your life and for your future—blaming yourself or your parents for your addiction traps you in the past. In recovery, you need to reserve all of your energy for the work ahead. Guilt just isn't worth your time right now.

Still, some people cling to the notion that drinking is a failure of willpower or a lack of moral fiber. Alcoholism, even today, remains to some an unspeakable, hidden, guilty subject. Drug dependence is likewise viewed as "something you'd stop if you had the character for it." Nonsense. As with any other disease, you are not responsible for catching it but you *are* responsible for doing something about it. Only one person in the world is responsible for that part: you.

The Goals of Recovery:
Seeing through the Eyes of Others

Once you've accepted addiction as a disease you may think it'll be clear sailing trying to convince everyone else and gain their support. Not so. But as you progress it will become easier to cope with and even influence the attitudes other people have about your addiction. They'll be learning along with you.

A family member or a friend—especially a drinking or drug-using friend—might not understand the true implications of your intention to give up your habit. And even if that person is not openly hostile to your decision, his or her response may well be confused and confusing. Here is a typical story, one I've heard many times:

I have an old friend I meet once a week for lunch and once or twice a month for dinner and a show, a movie, or a concert. Lunch used to mean one or two martinis and wine with the meal. Dinner meant the same, plus a drink or several after the show. The first time we got together after I quit drinking, I ordered plain tomato juice. Her eyebrows shot up but she didn't say anything at first. Then when I told her what I was doing she was terrific; her first words were supportive, encouraging. She said I was brave to face my problem and do something about it. But then, after two or three more get-togethers, I noticed she was drinking a little less comfortably, more self-consciously, and finally she asked me if I was really giving up drinking forever. Wouldn't I be able to control it, then have a drink once in a while? It was hard for me to tell her it didn't work that way. I could *see* her feeling sorry for me.

This kind of attitude can present serious dangers, especially in early recovery when all you have to show for your efforts is abstinence. You might start feeling sorry for yourself, too, for all you've "given up." You may begin to wonder whether kicking the habit is worth it if it means losing friends and giving up the fun. You might feel resentful: your friends can drink and not lose control, not be alcoholic. But in time you'll learn to work through it using the steps to recovery we will discuss, from treatment to twelve-step programs to specific coping techniques. The most reassuring thing is this: Dealing with these obstacles becomes less difficult as you learn, and you will eventually reach the stage of recovery where you don't *want* to drink or take drugs anymore.

One final point on this subject: It's a shame, but there are still physicians and psychiatrists who have not taken a particular interest in addictive diseases, who still have trouble accepting addiction as a disease. I think it's a crime. Some physicians and psychiatrists actually avoid treating addictions because they believe chemically dependent people are hard to treat and frequently relapse. If you encounter this attitude from someone in the healing profession, go straight to someone who *does* have experience in treating addiction.

The Goals of Recovery:
Recognizing Codependence

Of all the people you talk to about your addiction, your closest family members might present the greatest challenge of all. This happens for many reasons, among them what's known as "codependence." People are talking a lot about codependence nowadays, but not everyone understands exactly what it means. In short, codependence refers to the inevitable ill effects and emotional damage suffered by the families of the chemically dependent. As you recover, your family—indeed all of your important relationships—will undergo dramatic disruption as the patterns they had adopted in order to accommodate your habit begin to crumble. However favorable the eventual effects of your recovery will be, the initial disjunction can be unexpected and upsetting. Families need help in making their own recovery, and the best treatment programs not only include but *insist* on family therapy along with treatment of the alcoholic or drug abuser. (We'll discuss this in more detail in Chapter Six.)

This may come as a shock. You might have assumed that now that *you've* given up drinking or taking drugs all the troubles with your family or marriage will miraculously be fixed. There are no such miracles. In some marriages the commitment to recovery may bring resentment, bewilderment, and confusion. Often there's a lot of anger, too. In some people your recovery will create a strange kind of vacuum: spouses or family members who were devoted to their roles as Helper, Excuse-maker, and Comforter, to name a few, now feel "jobless." Perhaps they welcome your recovery but they feel ambivalent about the ways you, and therefore your relationships with them, have changed.

Lots of marriages and relationships, though, grow stronger through recovery. Married couples often discover, once the chemical barrier is removed, that they really *do* love each other, and this is a time when they're able to rediscover their shared love. The rebirth of intimacy and the faith couples have in each other can be a wellspring of help during the challenging time of early recovery. It is as if recovery has removed the layers of mistrust that have been built up by addiction, allowing old feelings of love to resurface and new ones to be born.

The Goals of Recovery: *Seeking Support*

Learning how to deal with the attitudes of those around you will become an integral part of your recovery, and one of the greatest sources of help for any recovering person is a twelve-step program. Alcoholics Anonymous is of course the best known, but there's also Cocaine Anonymous (CA), Alanon, Narcotics Anonymous (NA), and Alateen. All are modeled on

AA's Twelve Steps to Recovery. (See List of National Resources.) In meetings you'll meet people who have been through what you're experiencing. They'll give you sound advice. The feeling of support and acceptance a recovering person gets from a twelve-step program is inestimable. One recovering alcoholic patient recalls the first time she attended a twelve-step meeting, full of anxieties. What if she ran into someone she knew? What if people in the group looked down on her? She hadn't yet accepted her alcoholism as a disease so she was burdened by a great deal of shame. But here's what happened:

I did see people I recognized, people I never would have dreamed were alcoholics. There was a young man who worked at the grocery where I shopped—he knew me just well enough to say hello when I came in and that I preferred paper to plastic for bagging my groceries.

The next day when I went in to the grocery he gave me an enormous smile and said "Hi, how are you doing today?" His greeting was so warm and open and positive that I felt like I'd been hugged.

The Goals of Recovery:
Confronting Relapse

This is a subject we all wish we didn't have to write about, but the truth is that throughout early recovery the danger of relapse is everpresent. The body is being bombarded by the physical and chemical aftereffects of addiction; sometimes, for this purely physical reason, a person early in recovery can literally find it hard to think straight. Beyond that, in early recovery the changes are intense, piling on top of one another so quickly that it's hard to absorb the information all at once. The changes that come in a recovering person's personality, outlook, and belief in himself or herself haven't yet become incorporated completely. Being sober takes concentration at this point and it takes a lot of courage sometimes. This is why getting the right treatment is so important.

Both inpatient and outpatient treatment programs are designed to provide a protective environment, free of the personal and social factors that may have contributed to the original dependence. Generally, however, inpatient treatment or the intensive period of outpatient treatment don't last long enough for full recovery. For this reason, many treatment professionals like myself consider less intensive but continuing aftercare programs essential. But during the aftercare, you will be returning to the environment that fostered your dependency, and it is loaded with pressures, problems, and temptations. This is why most people who relapse do so during the first few months after completing inpatient treatment or the first phase of outpatient treatment. The biological effects of alcohol or drugs persist long after you might think they would: weeks or months after abstinence begins the body is making millions of adjustments, and it affects everyone differently. Still, there are patterns, and in this book we will sketch out for you what they are so that you can be prepared. If you're coming to this book as an addict who has already tried recovery once but not been able to stick with it, I think you'll find in this book the help you need to begin a successful recovery this time.

If this is your first time around or even your second, you should still know this: Relapse *can* be overcome. Although relapse is a real danger, especially in early recovery, you're not doomed to relapse. Many people never do. But second, don't think that relapse is something you can take lightly, that you can have one night of "fun" and then pick up where you left off. *Maybe* you can, but as one counselor puts it, "You may have one sober person inside you struggling to get out. You might even have two, three, or four. But you're not likely to have an infinite supply."

If you're in recovery, take it seriously. Take yourself seriously and get the help you need to begin living sober. It's worth it.

One final point: While therapy and the coping techniques of recovery all give you considerable control over how successfully and rapidly you recover, it's important to recognize and remember what you can control and what you can't. Don't set yourself up for failure by expecting everything to change for you all at once. You can control your own behavior, but *not* when you're drinking or taking drugs. You can't control what drink or drugs do to you. You can't control your feelings, but you *can* control how you act because of them. Very decidedly you can't control what other people feel or do or say. You *can* control your behavior toward them, which may influence what they feel or do, but don't count on it. This issue of control—a central issue in recovery—is perfectly summed up in the prayer with which many twelve-step groups end their meetings: "God grant me the serenity to accept what I cannot change, the courage to change what I can, and the wisdom to know the difference."

When you finally begin to achieve full recovery, you will then discover the gifts of recovery. Chief among these are discoveries about yourself as a functioning human being. Recovering people grow stronger, become physically healthier and mentally more competent. Gradually a recovering person will lose his fears about alcohol and drug related diseases while gaining concentration, memory, clarity, purpose, love, and spirituality (which doesn't necessarily mean religion).

The recovery process can be so rewarding that some of my patients are actually taken by surprise:

"I never thought I could look so good."

"I got paid yesterday, and I still have some money left."

"I actually enjoyed going to work again."

"Maybe I will go back to school."

"Life without nosebleeds—who would have thought it."

"No more lies."

"Sex. I forgot what it was like!"

"Somebody actually loves me."

Listen to their voices. Yours can join them. As difficult as the whole recovery process can be, you can—with perseverence, determination, the assistance of a good recovery program, and the support of your friends and loved ones—recover.

2

TREATMENT PROGRAMS:
WHAT TO EXPECT

AMONG THE FIRST QUESTIONS PEOPLE WONDER ABOUT WHEN they decide they need help are, "Must I be hospitalized?" and "What exactly goes on in treatment?" "Do I need detox?" "How do I know if a treatment program is good?" These are urgent and often unsettling questions, the answers to which are not nearly as intimidating or as mysterious as they may seem in the beginning.

First, in general, modern treatment for chemical dependence is based on two important principles: that addiction is a disease and that addicts can change their beliefs, attitudes, and behaviors. In general, the main goals of therapy are: first, abstinence from all mood-altering chemicals, and second, improvement of all other aspects of a person's life.

Specifically, a good treatment program aims to help the chemically dependent person:

1. recognize the illness and its implications;

2. admit that he or she needs help, accept that his or her illness cannot be "cured," and concentrate on learning to live with it in a constructive manner;

3. identify specifically what he needs to change in order to live with the illness in a constructive manner; and

4. translate that understanding into action—that is, make various changes necessary to develop a new way of life.

At Fair Oaks, we've organized these four points into the following "elements of recovery," which underscore the philosophy behind our Outpatient Recovery Center.

Finding the Best Help

So now, assuming you've made the decision to do something about your life, the first practical question is: which treatment center is for you? To evaluate any treatment center, you need to know not only what its goals are, but also how it goes about reaching them.

At Fair Oaks, the question of whether to choose residential (also called inpatient) or day- or evening-care (outpatient) treatment must be evaluated individually. Many people who have truly "hit bottom" just want to get away from the bad place they have been, accept shelter, and let someone else take over the burden. A former patient at Fair Oaks recalls that after several attempts at recovery on his own or through outpatient therapy, after being arrested several times and hospitalized more than once for injuries he suffered when he fell in the street while drunk and stoned, he finally turned to his parents and begged them to put him into an inpatient treatment where he wouldn't be able to do further damage to himself or others.

Unfortunately, not every addict realizes he needs help. The spouses, parents, other relatives, friends, and co-workers of these addicts often struggle with the very complex issue of getting this person into treatment. Several times I've been asked whether these addicts can be "committed" to a treatment facility, or forced to participate in a treatment program. While specific regulations vary from state to state, adult addicts, in

general, cannot be committed against their will or forced into
treatment unless the addict is in danger of killing himself or
someone else, or unless he has committed a crime (such as
driving while intoxicated). Parents of adolescent addicts usually
have more authority in committing substance-abusing teens under the age of eighteen.

Fortunately, the family, friends, and co-workers of an addict
do have an alternative to forced treatment: *intervention*. With
the help of a skilled counselor, the family, friends, and if possible
the co-workers all converge simultaneously on the addict. In
an orchestrated sequence, each person tells how the addict has
hurt them, how they've had to lie to protect the addict, and
how they've struggled with his addiction. Faced with this bar-
rage of honest accusations, even addicts in the deepest throes
of denial have recognized their addiction and entered voluntarily
into treatment. An intervention under the aegis of a skilled
counselor will get the addict into treatment about 80 to 90
percent of the time.

Now, I don't wish to make intervention seem like another
"day at the beach." It isn't; the emotions and accusations un-
leashed by such an experience can be very painful for all parties.
A qualified counselor, plus several hours of preparation, are
essential. The admissions office of the treatment facility, or, if
available, the employee assistance program (EAP) of the addict's
company should be able to assist with the intervention.

Inpatient or Outpatient?

There is no question you need inpatient treatment if your addiction is so longstanding that you have lost your outside "support structures" (your job, family, friends), or if you have been
using a chemical (such as cocaine or heroin) that causes withdrawal symptoms (such as vomiting, nausea, excessive anxiety,
irregular heartbeats) that may require medical attention. Addicts

may feel better and do better in an inpatient setting because it is safer and more protective—because it provides medical attention for detoxification or health problems, and because it separates you from temptations, from relapse-triggering people and events. It takes you out of the environment that has become associated with your habit, and away from pressures that could distract you from concentration on recovery—while placing you in an environment tailored to encourage recovery. It is a more all-encompassing and intense form of therapy, and it may be more effective in making sure you get safely through the first, most difficult few weeks.

In his book, *The Facts About Drugs and Alcohol*, Mark S. Gold, M.D., presents five questions that should be considered when evaluating an inpatient or outpatient program (Affirmative answers indicate that inpatient care is most likely the best choice):

1. Is the addict using large amounts of drugs, taking drugs on a nearly continuous basis, or using drugs intravenously? If so, the addict has a high risk of dying from an overdose; an inpatient program may literally save the addict's life.

2. Is the person addicted to more than one drug? Polyaddiction can be common, and usually occurs when a person uses one drug to counteract the effects of another.

3. Are severe psychiatric conditions (such as depression and anxiety disorders) and/or medical disorders (such as liver disorders or systemic infections) also present? These will require special medical attention.

4. Is the user completely incapable of taking care of himself, going to work, or interacting with other people?

5. Has the addict failed at previous outpatient treatment programs?

For many, however, outpatient therapy may be just as appropriate. You may feel more secure if you can stay on your job or be with your family in the evenings while you're going through structured outpatient treatment. A recent study showed that people who were hospitalized were more likely to complete the initial treatment, but after six months of treatment, those who were in outpatient treatment did just as well as the hospitalized group.

Cost is another factor in outpatient treatment's favor. Cost, because of different insurance plans and state regulations, is very difficult to determine, but many insurance plans will cover both inpatient and outpatient treatment. However, many insurance companies and/or the employee's company look more favorably on outpatient treatment because of its reduced cost. And for those without coverage, or for those who—for reasons of confidentiality—choose not to use insurance, the outpatient treatment is considerably less expensive.

Even for those who require inpatient treatment, a period of outpatient follow-up, or aftercare, is considered vital to long-term recovery. It's best to make your decision carefully, in consultation with family, physicians, and treatment counselors.

Choosing a treatment center requires thoughtful, informed consideration. Most experts on chemical dependence and treatment agree that a good treatment program contains the following components:

- **Crisis intervention**—the ability to get a seriously ill addict into treatment quickly with the help of concerned friends and family members.

- **Psychological testing** to find out if you also suffer from any mental or emotional disorders (especially depression and anxiety disorders) that may make treatment more difficult.

- **Medical and psychiatric care** for any health problems, or mental or physical problems, which could compro-

mise your recovery. Some treatment programs down-
play these other problems and focus exclusively on
addiction, believing that the other problems will disappear when the addiction is treated. While this approach
may work for some people, I have seen many patients
continue to need treatment for depression or panic attacks
years after their last substance abuse.

- **Social evaluation** to find out how your home life and
your work environment are affecting your dependence.

- **Licensed therapists** trained in various recognized methods of treatment. A good program includes not only
addiction counselors but also a psychiatrist or other medical doctor, a social worker, and skilled nurses.

- **Certified alcoholism counselors** licensed by the state,
who may well be recovering alcoholics or drug addicts
themselves. Someone who has been in your shoes is most
likely to succeed in breaking through your wall of denial.

- **Strong AA orientation**—the treatment program
should also approve of AA and related self-help groups,
help in introducing you to them, and encourage you to
stick with them.

- **Drug Screening**—I believe that a treatment program
must use urine testing to be truly successful. This is
controversial: some people object to drug testing because
it seemingly violates the trust that must develop between
the treatment provider and the recovering addict. My
answer to this objection is simple: I trust the recovering
person, I don't trust the disease. Addiction is a disease
that is built on deception; I've listened to countless addicts
brag about how they fooled other treatment centers, centers that didn't use drug testing. At my treatment program, any initial resistance an addict has to being tested
almost always dissipates with time. In fact most addicts

actually welcome the discipline that results from having to pass a drug test. Drug testing is important especially for outpatient programs that by their very nature lack the security of an inpatient program.

- **Aftercare** that focuses on keeping you active in a support group, and helping you strengthen your relationships with family, friends, and co-workers, and assisting your return to the workplace.

Understanding the Paradox

In order to begin a successful treatment program whether inpatient or outpatient, you must first understand a paradox.

The paradox is this: You must make the decision to recover and take responsibility for it—but at the same time you must "surrender" to the recovery process and to other people, to admit that you are powerless to control your disease.

Perhaps the best way to describe it is that it's like an exercise used by some psychotherapists to teach trust. The person stands with his back to a partner, and then is told to fall backward—to completely let go and fall. The person is told that the partner absolutely promises to catch him before he hits the ground.

Most people find this very difficult to do. Once they allow themselves to do it, however, they find it a remarkable and powerful experience. "Falling" becomes a foundation.

In essence, this is where therapy programs for chemical dependence really begin. You alone are responsible for the decision to "fall backward," but you must give yourself up in trust to those who promise to catch you.

Overcoming Denial

"I can stop whenever I want to."

"I'm not an alcoholic. I never take a drink before five o'clock."

"I'm just a recreational drug user."

"I only drink because of my job, I have to entertain clients and they expect it."

"Using drugs doesn't hurt anybody but me."

"I can quit anytime I want to."

Denial is a defense mechanism we all use, to a certain extent, to protect our image of ourself. It's usually linked to projection—throwing your own faults onto somebody else. "I didn't do it" and "It wasn't my fault" are denials; "If you hadn't forgotten to do this, then I wouldn't have done that" is projection.

But when you're chemically dependent, denial is not just a mechanism, it's a way of life. You refuse to own up to your actions and accept responsibility for them; also, you almost surely refuse to admit that you have a problem you can't solve. You deny that you've lost control.

The work of treatment involves confronting each one of your alibis and recognizing it for what it is. For instance, take the last example of denial: "I can quit any time I want to." This illusion of being able to control chemical abuse is universal among substance abusers. It's even more pronounced among young people, perhaps because they usually have a sense of omnipotence and immortality.

Even though they hear repeated warnings from parents, teachers, and the media, most young people literally believe, "It can't happen to me." Thus, they're amazingly unconcerned about their chances for getting hooked. Could this be because they haven't had a chance to experience many of the disasterous effects of heavy drinking or drug use? Maybe. Yet many older people, who have had plenty of these unpleasant experiences, keep right on abusing alcohol and drugs.

The euphoric effects of psychoactive chemicals temporarily bolster your pretense that you're not becoming dependent, that you can quit at any time. In spite of dramatic evidence—not being able to remember what happened last night, losing your job, seeing your family disintegrate, even being in a treatment program—you may stubbornly resist admitting that the root cause of your problems is chemical dependence.

Many people (and too many doctors, unfortunately) prefer to believe that chemical abuse is just a reflection of emotional problems or life stress, and that if those problems and stresses can be fixed, the chemical dependence will go away.

Getting Good Counsel

A keystone of many treatment programs, which I believe is an absolute essential, is the use of recovering people as counselors.

The most important reason is that recovering people really *understand* what you have been through and are going through. They have been there themselves. When they say, "I know how you feel" it's not just sympathy or empathy or somebody's attempt to soothe your concerns. It's a fact. At the same time, while a recovering counselor isn't trying to fool you, neither are you going to be able to fool him. A recovering therapist knows all the tricks and dodges and excuses and denials—having already used or heard them himself. He isn't going to be conned or sidetracked by tangential discussions of all your problems and "reasons" for drinking. He is best qualified to help you accept that it's not your troubled marriage or your job frustrations or your money worries that make you chemically dependent—it's your disease that makes you unable to cope with these other problems. He will not let you escape what he knows is necessary—to discard all the protective layers of denial and get down to the true core of yourself. What this means is putting an end to the defenses or excuses you have used for your be-

havior in order to protect your idealized image of yourself—
and discover the unidealized real person, which usually, in fact,
turns out to be a much better one.

It also could be called redirecting yourself from inward to
outward: learning to stop thinking so much about yourself and
to start thinking more about the world around you. The great
American psychologist William James called this transformation
"ego deflation at depth." Some mystics call it "being grounded"
or "centering down."

Recovering people describe it more simply as feeling together
or having peace of mind. Most importantly, when they lose
their egocentricity they also lose their compulsion to drink.
Constantly confronted by counselors who by their own experience know there is no alternative except sobriety, the chemically dependent person eventually has to confront for himself
the reality that there is no alternative. As one experienced counselor has said, chemically dependent people "love recovery"
once they know there's no alternative.

Using Group Therapy

While individual counseling is valuable, the group experience
within a treatment program is central to the success of treatment. Just as it is impossible to lie to a counselor who is a
recovering addict, it is equally impossible to get away with
deceit in a peer group. And of course, cutting through the lies
and the denial is the big issue. When others with your problem
are in daily contact with you, when they get to know you and
begin to talk to you about yourself, they are in the best position
to see through the veneer to what is really there—and to do it
with compassion. At the same time, the sense that you, in turn,
are able to help them nourishes your self-esteem and your sense
of your own worth as a human being. The basic message learned

from over a half-century of AA is that mutual concern and mutual help are powerful tools.

The issue in the group process is that in order to recover, you have to face certain realities which the group can help you to see and accept. One of these is that the person you have been since you became chemically dependent is a false self—egocentric, selfish, deceptive to others and to yourself. A second reality is that the only alternative to recovery is further deterioration—and ultimately, death. A third reality, and a cheering one, is that your "addicted self" is masking your real self, which is honest, kind, and genuinely open to others. Recovery involves unmasking that inner, real self.

Overcoming "Terminal Uniqueness"

Something counselors always notice when a new member enters a therapy group is that he tends to sit apart, to distance himself from the others. The counselors know that what is going on in the new member's mind is something like this: "I don't really belong with this group. They're alcoholics and addicts; I just have a drinking problem." Sometimes the thought is, "These guys are amateurs: beer drinkers and pot smokers. They don't realize cocaine is the only way to go." Or: "These poor people really think some mysterious 'power' is going to solve all their problems. Not me. I'm going to do it myself. I've made up my mind; and when I make up my mind, nothing stops me."

All of this is what I call "terminal uniqueness." Nearly every chemically dependent person starts therapy thinking he is somehow very different from everybody else. Any treatment program that doesn't overcome this terminal uniqueness will usually fail.

One of the first of many jobs—the "work"—to be done in therapy is to shake off that notion and begin to identify with the rest of the group. Of course, each one of us has our individual character, history, and personality. But we are all exactly the same in one respect: we're all suffering from the same disease. The woman who has come for treatment because her husband threatens to leave her and take the kids is in the same boat as the man who beat his wife every time he got drunk. The twenty-year-old who hasn't been able to keep a job because he was always high at work is very similar to the sixty-year-old woman whose hands tremble and whose liver is scarred—the younger man just hasn't had time to get there yet. The executive on cocaine is brother to the nineteen-year-old girl who has been drinking a couple of pints of gin a day.

Drug addicts, even more than alcoholics, tend to think of themselves as special, glamorous, and "cool."

Writer Gail Regier described it vividly in *Harper's* magazine:

Real users . . . are different from the straight people. We are special, we are more free. We are spiritual adventurers. When I was twenty-four, which was not so long ago, my friends and I thought nothing was more hip than drugs, nothing more depraved, nothing more elemental. When we were messed up, we seemed to become exactly who we were, and what could be more dangerous and splendid. Other vices made our lives more complicated. Drugs made everything simple and pure. . . .

Some of the users I knew were people with nothing left to lose. The rest of us were in it a little for the money, more than a lot for the nights we would drive to one place after another, in and out of people's parties, looking for a connection. It was a kind of social life, and we weren't in a hurry.

What we had in common was drugs. Getting high bound us together against outsiders, gathered us into a common purpose. No one else understood us and we understood each other so well.

What the therapeutic group can do—once the newcomer sees that connection—is to provide that same common purpose and understanding, but in a positive, health-giving way.

Your deluded sense of uniqueness might express itself in anger as you begin to realize that for whatever reason, you have a disease that you can't cure, that you *don't* have the power to overcome by yourself: "Why me?" the chemically dependent often asks fiercely.

How you answer the "why me?" question depends in large measure on your personality and on what kind of help you get. One answer is, Why not you? It's just the luck of the draw. Somebody else may have something far worse. An even better answer, which treatment can help you accept, is that the life changes that come with true recovery give you the opportunity to make something even better of your life than you might have otherwise. For many people it can be like the heightened awareness and appreciation of life that comes from a close brush with death, or with recovery from a life-threatening illness like cancer.

Losing "terminal uniqueness" isn't really a loss. When you accept that you and all other people with a dependency disease are alike, then you may begin to see that the fates or God or whatever haven't singled you out. You will even begin to feel compassion for others with the disease. And with compassion comes a reduction in the selfish behavior so typical of addiction.

Expressing Real Feelings

One way the therapeutic process and the group can help is to encourage and guide you in expressing your *real* feelings. You may be angry, for example, but given a chance to talk about it and given the right questions to answer, you may discover that the anger is really a mask for pain and hurt. When you feel you

want a drink or a drug and you talk about it you may learn that
it's not really a chemical you want, it's approval, or job recognition, or the love of someone you've lost: the craving is just
a habitual, knee-jerk reaction to unhappiness, loneliness, and
feelings of inadequacy. Because once upon a time you took a
drink to soothe some pain, and because your disease then made
it pure habit to take a drink when something hurt, you do it
automatically. You've completely forgotten—or you never
quite learned—that it *doesn't* remove the pain. You haven't yet
accepted the fact that it just puts the pain into brief oblivion;
afterward it's still there, and added to it is whatever damage
you did by drinking or taking drugs.

But in therapy, when you think about taking a drink or a
drug, someone can help you "talk the drink through." That
means describing and *remembering truthfully* just exactly what
will happen if you take the drink or the drug: how at first it
will make you feel comfortable again, then foggy-headed, then
hungry for more of the drug or drink, then drunk or stoned,
then hung over or crashing, then guilty and miserable—and
without any relief from whatever pain you *thought* made you
take the drink or drug in the first place. When you can go
through this entire exercise honestly, and recognize that your
pattern is consistent—one drink or one joint is *never* enough—
then you are beginning to dismantle your denial of the chemical's tyranny over you. Then it's only a short step away from
the rock-bottom admission that you don't drink to ease the
pain, or to be sociable, or to relax from the day's stresses: you
drink *to get drunk* or you take drugs *to get high*.

Then you can ask yourself what good does that do you? This
exercise can also bolster your effort to learn another essential
truth: the bad part was always far worse than the good part was
good. Many chemically dependent people cling to the pleasant
memories associated with drinking or taking drugs, and easily
forget the negative side. "Talking the drink through" is a way
of reminding yourself that the sociability of drinking—the taste
of the fine wine, the connections between beer and baseball, or

cocaine and sophisticated night life—were brief, fleeting, and overwhelmed in importance by the misery and grief that went with them. Eventually you will discover how easy it is to have a good time without chemicals; for the moment, it's necessary only to remind yourself that the "good time" was really a bad time.

When denial really starts to unravel you will begin to find it impossible to say, "I can quit anytime" to a group of other people who are living proof that they couldn't do it either. And then it also becomes considerably harder to keep believing it yourself.

When the alibi system begins to fall apart, many other things begin to happen and are helped along by the treatment process. When you stop denying that you can't control your chemical dependence, then you also begin to see that you can't control many other things, especially the behavior of other people. When you stop denying that you alone must take the responsibility for continuing the work of therapy after you finish the program, then you may stop blaming other people for your drinking problem in the first place. When you really accept that you are like all other chemical dependents in your helplessness against the disease of dependence, you will stop dwelling on the real or imagined hurts or deprivations or failures that you used to blame for your behavior; you will begin to stop feeling sorry for yourself.

Providing Moment-to-Moment Answers

The treatment program, especially the group activities, will help you with the immediate moment-to-moment discomforts of recovery. To the practical questions of what you will do with your hands, what you will substitute *right now* for the glass or the needle, the answer will be a ballpoint pen and a notebook for keeping a daily journal; books; conversation (about things other than where you're going to make a connection or excuses for why you didn't show up for work); soft drinks or seltzer water; food . . . and for many, coffee and cigarettes.

In Montreal, in the middle of a 1988 Alcoholics Anonymous convention, the demand for coffee and cigarettes was so tremendous that the participating hotels literally ran out of supplies. I overheard one cab driver remarking wryly, "Looks like these AA folks just traded one addiction for a couple of others."

Are caffeine and nicotine really substitute addictions? Yes, they certainly can be. Coffee, generally harmless in small amounts, may cause jitteriness, heart pounding, and insomnia when used heavily. Cigarettes are notoriously addictive, and have extremely serious long-term effects on the lungs and the cardiovascular system. Nevertheless, most of today's treatment programs will allow you to drink coffee and smoke tobacco. Why? Because these substances will do you far less immediate harm than what you have been using. Neither one, even used to excess, will cause you to drive down the wrong side of the road, neglect your children, squander your paycheck in a day, or lose your job through incompetence. Neither is illegal. A coffee-and-cigarette addict may not be in top physical or mental shape, but at least he can function adequately in day-to-day living.

However, I do not mean to minimize the well-established health risks of tobacco. Recently, with over 80 percent of all people in recovery currently classified as nicotine-dependent (compared to only 28 percent of the general population), a growing number of treatment professionals have begun to address this problem. In my own program at the Outpatient Recovery Center, I have recently introduced a series of lectures on nicotine dependence. These lectures stress that cigarette smoking and recovery do not go hand in hand, and that recovering individuals should at the very least begin to contemplate quitting smoking.

Please note that *no* reliable treatment program will let you substitute tranquilizers for alcohol, or barbiturates or alcohol for cocaine. Some recovering drug users are surprised that they must give up not only their drug, but drinking as well. "But I don't have a problem with alcohol, just cocaine," they protest. The point is that any of these powerful habit-forming substances is just as dangerous to your well-being as the one it replaces. Remember, the goal of recovery is to live life comfortably *without addicting chemicals*.

That is one of the reasons why at Fair Oaks, and at many other treatment centers, alcoholics and drug users are treated together in the same environment and in the same groups. This was not always the case; separate treatment for different types of chemical dependence used to be standard. Partly this was rooted in the traditions of Alcoholics Anonymous, which considered itself a society dedicated to helping alcoholics and alcoholics only. In recent years, however, AA has changed its position somewhat. (This will be discussed in the section on twelve-step programs.) At Fair Oaks, our experience has shown us that many drug users are alcoholics, too. While certain details of treatment might be influenced by the particular kind of chemical dependence, the goals of recovery and the means of achieving them are virtually identical.

Many people are surprised by the classification of alcohol as a drug, and some have asked me why this book covers both alcohol and drug recovery. Alcohol *is* a drug—its primary active ingredient, ethanol, is a central nervous system depressant; taken in high doses, ethanol acts as an anesthetic; in low doses it helps to break down inhibitions and social restraints. Alcohol and illegal drug use go hand in hand: not every alcoholic has used cocaine, but every cocaine addict I know has also used alcohol. So many times I've heard patients describe their typical cocaine binge, how this binge would always start with a few beers or shots of whiskey, only to hear these same patients argue that they don't have a problem with alcohol. They may not be alcoholics, but alcohol acts as a gateway, an enemy agent that weakens their defenses against drugs. This is why at Fair Oaks we stress that all addicts, even cocaine and heroin addicts, must avoid all mood-altering substances, including alcohol.

Acknowledging Warped Relationships

Treatment soon reveals that your chemical dependence has fundamentally warped and skewed your closest relationships—and that abstinence will produce no miracles (although work and goodwill might). If you're married, both you and your spouse have been affected—you by the chemical dependence itself, and your mate by the destructive ways that dependence changed you.

Then your drinking or drug taking stops.

What does this mean for the relationship? Only that the focus is lost, that the chemical is no longer the focal point of life. Nothing else happens automatically. Trust that was lost does not come back just because chemical abuse stops. Just as a history of unfulfilled promises has damaged your spouse's trust, a new history has to come into play in order to rebuild it.

Longstanding anger, disappointment, and mistrust don't disappear automatically just because you've stopped drinking.

Strong feelings that both of you repressed while you were drinking or taking drugs may now *want* to come cascading out—but the lines of communication have been cut. An addict in early recovery, and that addict's spouse, are two blind people without a road map. Yet whether they like it or not, these two blind people are trailblazers. Because they need to build a whole new relationship, they are forced to feel their way into unknown territory.

Mapping Out New Relationships

To help people draw road maps to renewed relationships, the most effective treatment programs not only suggest but urge participation in therapy for spouses or other closely affected family members, and may recommend participation in a special support group such as Alanon or Adult Children of Alcoholics (ACOA). As we will discuss in detail in Chapter Six, chemical dependence is a "family disease" from which no one is immune. Not just spouses but children are damaged—the latter, in some ways, even more severely. The damage to your family does not correct itself merely because you abstain or even recover fully. Your family members have their *own* particular needs. Treatment and recovery must also meet these needs in appropriate ways.

Surviving Change

We've seen that recovery involves massive change—and of course the words "massive change" are intimidating. Most people are frightened by change, even if they hope or believe the change will be for the better. For the chemically dependent person, change is the only road to survival. And in a good treatment program, change will not be imposed on you; you will be guided and helped to make changes yourself. Both counselors and peer groups will be there to support you as this happens.

Changes can feel a lot like pure loss. The first, most obvious, and most dramatic loss comes with abstinence. What most people feel at the beginning of abstinence is not only relief, accomplishment, something new and hopeful, but also a *sense of emptiness* that can be as strong as grief. You are, in fact, losing a lot of things. You are losing a crutch, a kind of friend, something to turn to when everything becomes too much to handle.

You wonder where you are going to turn now. You are also losing a lot of the structure of your daily life, which has consisted so much of getting supplies of your chemical of choice, preparing, drinking—all the rituals that have become as deeply rooted in your pattern of living as sleep, work, and food. What can you reach out to *psychologically* instead of a glass or a joint? How do you keep busy during the time you used to be busy drinking or drugging?

In treatment you will find the answers.

Eventually, when you are out of therapy, you will fill the holes with work, pleasure, exercise, real friendships based on something other than just using together, a true enjoyment of life. Meanwhile, during therapy, you will also fill the gap with the companionship of your peer group and your counselors. You will fill the empty space by sharing experiences with others who have the same problems, by occupying your mind and your time with learning how to grow and how to cope. You will slowly get past the grieving, and gradually recognize that you are giving up some extremely dubious "advantages" in exchange for something of real value—a life worth living.

Restoring Your Support

The process of rehabilitation and recovery is something like restoring a painting by an old master which has over the years been retouched, varnished, painted over, until layer after layer of paint, dirt and darkness have obscured the brilliance and beauty of the original. Each layer has to be stripped away to get to the true painting.

So in rehabilitation you are stripped of the layers of thought and behavior that built up during your chemical dependence: these layers of "dirt" include self-pity, guilt, blaming others, self-deceit, denial, loneliness, shame, confusion, defensiveness, resentment, grandiosity, manipulativeness, and cynicism. Underneath is the true person you are capable of being, one who is open, optimistic, able to befriend others and to laugh.

An effective treatment program, in short, is designed to take away the *faulty* support system of denial and drink or drugs, and to replace it with a new one that works. It brings about a seismic change in your life-style: from the old reward system of chemically induced highs, to a new one based on inner growth, spiritual values, and honest relationships.

Support Groups

When you leave a good rehab program, whether inpatient or outpatient, you will be encouraged to join a support group.

The whole modern system of rehabilitation from alcohol and drug abuse began with the birth of Alcoholics Anonymous (AA) in the mid-1930s. This organization produced a group of alcoholics who rejected the prevailing view of alcoholism as a symptom of underlying psychological problems. From the beginning, these pioneers insisted that alcoholics had something physically, permanently "different" about their personal biochemistry—a built-in susceptibility to dependence on alcohol—so that their only real hope for recovery lay in total abstinence.

Another way of putting it (and the statements are true for other chemical dependencies as well as alcoholism) can be found in an article I co-wrote with Norman Miller, M.D., Mark Gold, M.D., and A. Carter Pottash, M.D.: "Most individuals, whether alcoholic or not, appear to consume alcohol for the same reasons, i.e., happiness or sadness, success or failure, weddings or divorces, birth or death, or simply to enhance social interaction. . . . An extremely crucial and difficult notion to comprehend is that a certain portion of the population drinks too much alcohol in the presence of these life events only incidentally. The reason alcoholics drink is that alcohol affects them differently and apparently provides them with an unusual psychic reinforcement that those without a vulnerability to alcohol do not need. In short, life problems, emotions, circumstances, and events may lead to drinking but do not explain abnormal drinking. These life problems are the frequent consequences of abnormal drinking."

In recent years, other support groups have been formed along the lines of AA: Narcotics Anonymous, Cocaine Anonymous, and Drugs Anonymous. Your counselor can advise you about which group or groups would be most appropriate for you. Many drug abusers go to AA because it is the oldest and most well-established of the self-help organizations, or because it has more convenient meetings and more groups in the area. Others go to AA because they have an alcohol problem as well as a drug habit. Some people find it valuable to attend both AA and CA.

For some years, AA appeared to treat people with more than one addiction as unwelcome intruders on a closed fellowship. Some people were publicly asked to leave a meeting or not to come back; others were accused of "showing off" if they introduced themselves with the phrase "I am an alcoholic and a drug addict."

More recently, AA—or at least many individual groups in AA—have become more accepting and open to people with mixed addictions (both alcohol and drugs), if not quite so welcoming to those with a drug problem only. Many members openly champion the right of such people to attend AA, citing the stated tradition that "You are a member of AA if you say you're a member." One must, however, be prepared for the possibility that a particular AA group will not make you feel comfortable; the solution is to find another group that will. In fact, people are always advised to attend meetings of various different groups in order to find one that "fits" best.

Support groups vary widely in their membership; some are intended to meet the special needs of younger or older people, or people who share a cultural style or even a particular language. Some groups number in the hundreds; others may be as small as a dozen or so.

Meeting regularly, the support group provides an atmosphere in which recovering people can share their experiences, their fears and despairs, and also their strengths and hopes. The sponsor system allows you to pair up with a person who has been in recovery for long enough to guide you through each of the steps, to advise you, to listen to you, and to back you up when things are going badly. Participating regularly in a group reduces your sense of isolation and loneliness, while fostering a powerful and necessary dependence on the group and its members. Hearing others speak at a meeting is often a moving emotional experience that makes a permanent impression, speeding your own personal growth and change.

Treatment programs emphasize AA as a source of help, and as a lifelong resource after intensive treatment is over, for a very simple reason: what works works. The popular statement is, "There's no guarantee that AA will lick your problem, but it's almost guaranteed that you won't lick your problem without AA."

AA's record of success is so well known that if you resist going to meetings, your therapist is apt to interpret this as a sign of a deep denial of your problem. While you may feel you have valid "reasons" for not wanting to go—it's time-consuming, the meeting hours aren't convenient, you've never been a "group type of person," you're afraid you might meet someone you know, and so on—none of these is really a valid reason not to try AA. One member of an AA group commented, "I thought I didn't have time for all those meetings. Then I realized that a meeting only lasts an hour, and I had been wasting five times that much every day in drinking."

There's No
Fairy-Tale Ending

If your partner joins Alanon, does that guarantee that the two of you will live happily ever after? No, it's not that easy. The two of you may have a rocky road ahead of you, even if you're both seeking help. Of all the "losses" that accompany recovery, the most serious and real is the potential loss of a valued relationship within your own family—divorce, separation from your children, perhaps breaking off with your parents.

Chemical dependence produces extremely unnatural situations that work against marriage partnerships and family ties.

Howard and Sharon, a long-married couple, ran into trouble when Howard took the advice of his AA sponsor and literally insisted on getting rid of "all the liquor and pills in the house." Sharon, a skilled cook who liked to entertain, was incredulous and outraged. She couldn't believe Howard would never again allow her to serve wine to their own dinner guests, or eggnog to the neighbors on New Year's Eve. Howard wouldn't even consider the compromise of letting her buy drinks for established occasions, such as family holiday meals or the weekly game of cards. Sharon felt trapped. Did "recovery" mean that she and Howard could no longer have a social life?

Josh, a young computer programmer, had been snorting many lines of cocaine a day before he came to our Fair Oaks program. Over the course of three years, as his drug habit grew, he lost all interest in his work: he regularly showed up late, missed important meetings, muffed routine jobs, and eventually got fired. At home, too, Josh let everything slide: he no longer mowed the lawn, helped with the kids, ate dinner with the family, or even had sexual relations with his wife, Cindy. He became, in effect, a sick and irresponsible child. Cindy, whose maternal instinct was strong, slipped into "mothering" him without fully realizing it. Gradually she assumed the role of sole head of their household. When Josh lost his job she became the chief breadwinner, too. Under these conditions, their marriage was no longer a partnership.

When Josh broke the pattern by entering treatment and beginning recovery, Cindy expected to be overjoyed—but she was not. Instead, she felt suddenly empty—as though she had lost a child (and indeed she had!). To her it seemed that after spending enormous time, effort, and love supporting Josh, she now had nothing to show for it: Josh was betraying her, turning elsewhere for the support he needed. Wounded by the rejection, she began to think that there was nothing left for her in this relationship.

Richard, whose wife Lorraine was undergoing treatment at Fair Oaks for her alcoholism, also ran into a road block. For sixteen years Richard had been not only the family's sole wage earner, but also the only real parent to his and Lorraine's four children. On one level Richard resented this double burden, but on another level he accepted and even enjoyed everyone's heavy dependence on him: it nourished his idea of himself as the strong one, the head of the family. When Lorraine began to recover, she acquired a new, more "liberated" view of herself. Richard's initial response was fury and rejection.

Sometimes not even counselors or mutual-help groups can guide a troubled couple toward solutions, either to such practical problems as the disposal of liquor or to the deeper problems of a warped relationship. Sometimes it is too late. But many times—when the nondependent partner participates in Alanon, perhaps more often than not—the recovery process leads both partners to the kind of growth and self-discovery that makes each a stronger and better mate. When the nondependent partner is able to remain loyal and supportive, recovery can bring a couple closer than they have been since their marriage began.

How Long Will a
Treatment Program Last?

The length of individual treatment programs vary considerably: inpatient programs usually last four weeks while outpatient programs may last up to two years. I classify the program that I run at The Outpatient Recovery Center as a one-year program, divided into three phases:

Phase I is an initially intense period consisting of four to five sessions per week, with each session lasting up to six hours. Patients may attend day or evening sessions, usually depending on their employment status. Phase I usually lasts eight weeks, and is designed to help patients through the early stages of abstinence and withdrawal, and to guide them toward a lifetime of recovery. Individual and group counseling covers all areas of recovery, including substance-abuse education, the physical and psychiatric affects of substance abuse, family therapy, proper nutrition, and employment counseling.

Phase II consists of twice weekly sessions over a four-week period. During this phase patients are assisted in their return to normal life, and prepared for the obstacles they will face.

Phase III begins the aftercare section of our program and lasts for the remainder of the first year. Patients meet in once-a-week sessions and are counseled in coping with specific situations (weddings, funerals, etc.) that invariably arise. In addition, participation in regular AA meetings is encouraged strongly—in fact, several AA groups meet on our premises.

THE HOT SEAT

Toward the end of many rehabilitation programs, including
Phase I of my program at Fair Oaks, there is an experience
known as "peer evaluation," more wryly referred to by patients
as "the hot seat." It is the time when you and your group will
really examine carefully the negative behavior and personality
traits that built up during your time of dependence—and evaluate how far you have come in getting rid of them or out-
growing them.

The idea is to gather up all the knowledge of the recovering
person that has been accumulating bit by bit through group
sessions, and to confront that person with that knowledge in
an intense session in which all the power—and caring—of the
group is concentrated.

First the person who is preparing to complete the program
tells his or her "life story" to the whole group. The following
day is the evaluation: the group sits in a large circle surrounding
the subject, and one by one they read their evaluations of the
person's progress and current state, using a prepared checklist.
Each group member also reads aloud a personal letter to the
subject.

The evaluators are asked to mark their checklists on a "today"
basis—not how the person used to be but how he is right now.
They are instructed not to moralize about the past in their letters
but to write "with love and concern."

The checklist covers every important point in the recovery
process; anyone who has a lot of check marks has more work
to do; anyone with only a few can be considered well along in
recovery.

The Peer Evaluation Checklist

Minimizes the disease of chemical dependence.
Life story lacks honesty.
Lacks commitment to recovery.
Blames others for own shortcomings.
Is complying with treatment only to satisfy others.
Sees self as victim/filled with self-pity.
Too many concerns outside treatment.
Overly defensive with confronted/unsurrendered.
Overvalues self.
Talks too much/poor listener.
Wants to do it alone, will not ask for help.
Constantly testing, breaking rules.
Hides true feelings/wears a mask.
Hidden anger/resentful.
Not in touch with feelings.
Hypocritical/talks the talk, doesn't walk the walk.
Perfectionist.
Too serious, no sense of humor.
Does not trust others.
Preoccupied with past/unduly guilty.
Projects a gloomy future.
Isolated/avoids others.
Too passive, doesn't assert self enough.
Low self-esteem.

If this evaluation is done, as it should be, with a genuine concern for the subject's recovery, it is extraordinarily effective. When twenty people who obviously care about you tell you that self-pity is your worst fault, it's very difficult to keep on denying it. When twenty people are taking the risk of being completely honest with you, knowing that you may be angry at them for it but daring to do it because they know it will help, it's hard to keep lying to them or to yourself.

When you have at least made a dent in this list of denials, excuses, and evasions, when you finally stop denying that drink or drugs were ruining your life and the lives of others and eventually would have killed you, then you are coming even closer to the time when you can say not only "I don't drink or take drugs anymore" but you can even say, "I don't *need* or *want* to drink or take drugs anymore."

The Importance of Aftercare

The bridge between abstinence and the lifetime of recovery is a formal aftercare program; the guardian of that change is twelve-step participation.

Aftercare should be a commitment that extends a minimum of eight weeks after discharge from rehabilitation. In some centers aftercare may last up to two years, and in other centers the recovering alcoholic or addict returns for week-long refresher periods on a regular basis. Theoretically, aftercare could extend for as long as a person feels it is needed; the only concern is that it is possible to become too dependent on aftercare and to cling to it past the point where one should be more emotionally and psychologically self-sustaining. The essence of an aftercare program is to help the recovering person learn new behavior and to practice it with other recovering people in a controlled environment. Study after study has demonstrated without any doubt that intense involvement in aftercare appears critical, and that relapse rates are dramatically higher among those who do not have aftercare.

During and after aftercare, virtually all physicians and rehabilitation centers urge—sometimes even insist—on participation in a twelve-step group. In fact, there was no so-called epidemic of treatment centers until the AA support network developed effectively throughout the country. It was felt in the profession that without some follow-up support, treatment-center work would not last and would be almost a waste of time. Today, certain rehabilitation centers that incorporate AA (or NA or CA) into their treatment programs estimate that up to 80 percent of alcoholics are still sober two years after leaving treatment; whereas those rehabilitation centers that *don't* include these techniques may have lower success rates.

Because of its conviction that the alcoholic is powerless against the effects of drink, AA rejects both willpower and insight as the essential forces for change. Instead, it encourages its members to depend on one another and to rely on a supportive power—the so-called "higher power"—outside of themselves. AA systematizes its approach in its twelve steps, reprinted below.

Step One: "We admitted we were powerless over alcohol—that our lives had become unmanageable."

Step Two: "Came to believe that a Power greater than ourselves could restore us to sanity."

Step Three: "Made a decision to turn our will and our lives to the care of God as we understood Him."

Step Four: "Made a searching and fearless moral inventory of ourselves."

Step Five: "Admitted to God, to ourselves, and to another human being, the exact nature of our wrongs."

Step Six: "Were entirely ready to have God remove all these defects of character."

Step Seven: "Humbly asked Him to remove our shortcomings."

Step Eight: "Made a list of all persons we had harmed, and became willing to make amends to them all."

Step Nine: "Made direct amends to such people wherever possible, except when to do so would injure them or others."

Step Ten: "Continued to take personal inventory and when we were wrong promptly admitted it."

Step Eleven: "Sought through prayer and meditation to improve our conscious contact with God as we understood Him, praying only for knowledge of His will for us and the power to carry that out."

Step Twelve: "Having had a spiritual awakening as a result of these steps, we tried to carry this message to alcoholics, and to practice these principles in all our affairs."

The Twelve Steps, reprinted with permission of Alcoholics Anonymous World Services Incorporated.

Embracing AA

It is useful to recount the twelve steps, although they may not be very meaningful to anyone who is beginning to confront a decision to seek treatment. In addition, newcomers typically back away when they first read steps two and three, which seem to imply either a heavy dose of religion or something impractically spiritual.

Many people, in fact, shy away from AA because they have an antipathy to religion or a distaste for prayer or worship. Some AA groups are indeed very religiously oriented. Others, however, are not. In such groups, it's suggested that nonreligious people think of their "higher power" as the power of group support, or indeed as anything greater than themselves. The meeting might open or close with a prayer, but the leader will introduce the prayer by inviting "those who wish to join us." In most AA groups it is common to hear people express their doubts about the existence of God; it is also common to hear people acknowledge that they feel some new, unidentified source of power or meaning in life.

It is difficult to describe this power without sounding mystical or magical. Few people have been able to explain it, nor is the power always apparent the first time you attend a meeting or even the second or third time. But many AA members testify that not very long after beginning to attend meetings they begin to feel "at home" and as if they "belong," and that the people in their groups, although still strangers, are the best friends they have in the world. Much of this comes from AA's ready acceptance of new members, from your instant recognition that you don't have to feel ashamed or apologetic in this group, and from your realization that all the others have gone through what you have gone through and are succeeding in recovery. It's reassuring to hear group members talk about their past and present, and to hear that much of their effort in recovery consists of highly practical behavior—not mystical revelations or divine intervention. Finally, involvement in a group is one of the best ways of overcoming denial: every member of a twelve-step group introduces himself or herself by first name only, adding "I'm an alcoholic (or drug addict)." Hearing this over and over takes away some of the awkwardness and strangeness, and makes it not only easier to say but easier to admit to yourself. And admission of the true nature of your problem is the first step toward overcoming it.

Also, going to meetings can help solve one of the biggest problems you'll encounter in early recovery: what you're going to do with the time you used to spend at your addiction. If you're accustomed to coming home after work and reaching for the bottle, or heading for a bar or a fellow drug user's house, you'll be casting around for ways to occupy yourself at first. Treatment planners understand this and help guide you to pleasant and productive ways to enjoy or use your spare time. But especially in the beginning, having a meeting to go to at seven

P.M. or on Saturday morning provides structure and security—
something to look forward to as well as to lean on.

Recovery Is Work

One final comment: No matter which treatment program you
choose, you'll be compensating for abstinence and your various
other "losses" with *work*. Treatment programs *are* work.
Twelve-step programs are work—which is why nobody talks
about "doing" the twelve steps. They talk about "working"
them. You will discover one striking difference between the
work of recovery and the "busyness" that took up so much
time and effort when you were chemically dependent. Back
then, you were just *using up* time. Now, you will be *using* it.
You will be busy breaking down your denial of your problem,
discovering hidden resources you didn't know you had, learning
to look beyond yourself to other people, and finding out that
being honest is not only possible, but emancipating.

3
DEALING WITH THE DOWN SIDE
OF RECOVERY

The cocaine withdrawal had been quick, but the Valium was a night-mare. I would sleep maybe seven hours a week and eat very little . . . I would go through three or four T-shirts a night that were soaked with sweat. It was absolute, sheer hell . . . I had these monumental panic attacks in the middle of the night. I would be walking Madison Avenue at two in the morning with tremendous physical pain and absolute panic. I was hanging onto parking meters to keep from falling down. I wanted to run but I didn't know where to run to. It got so bad that I checked into a hospital . . . I slowly began to get better. Of course, time was a factor. As time goes along, you start to get better.
—Jim Jensen, a TV news reporter in New York City
and a former patient at Fair Oaks.*

REHABILITATION FROM CHEMICAL DEPENDENCE IS A LOT LIKE rehabilitation from a serious trauma such as a spinal cord injury or the loss of a leg. It can be painful, and it is definitely work. The victim of a physical trauma has to go through many sessions of exercise, retraining wasted muscles, stretching and learning to move again, slowly and painfully learning to stand upright, to walk with the support of parallel bars, and then crutches, perhaps even a prosthetic limb. There are difficult moments, and sometimes the process seems never-ending; to keep going requires regular reminders of the tremendous benefits to be achieved.

The same is true of the person trying to recover from the trauma of chemical dependence, with the added complication of having to deal with the self-inflicted waste of life, damage to the family, job and money problems, guilt and longing. There will be difficult moments, even days, times when you

*Jim Jensen, "A Veteran TV Anchorman's Toughest Story Was His Own—He Had to Beat Drugs and Depression," *People Weekly*, September 4, 1989, pp. 67–73.

feel defeated. This chapter will be about these times, the down side of recovery.

I remember a conversation with a patient named Don a few months after his initial treatment. Don had been a "model" patient, one who had really worked hard at his recovery. But on that day, Don hardly looked like a model patient. I didn't need a medical degree to see his pain and anger.

> I don't get it. I really don't. Everything in my life seems so hopeless, I'm a failure at everything. At least when I was drinking I knew I was good at something: 'There goes Don, boy, he sure can drink like a fish.' Now, I don't even do that! I never thought that recovery meant feeling so lousy. I still hate my job. I like to think—I used to think— that I was a creative person, but any idiot could do my job. My ex-wife barely talks to me and my kids still don't trust me—they still instinctively pull away when I try to hug them—they still hate me. What good am I? Now you tell me that I'm suffering from depression. No kidding. You told me that it was going to be tough, but not like this. I mean, what's the point?

I asked him if he had had a drink. He said, "No, but—"

"That *is* the point," I interrupted. "In my eyes that makes you pretty successful. Before, well, I don't have to tell you what you would have done."

I'd like to say that my conversation with Don changed his life and inspired him to achieve new heights—but that's not how it works. A few months of sobriety allowed Don's depression to be seen as a clinical condition apart from his alcoholism. In addition, Don faced many other challenges: a career crisis, seeing his children only every other weekend, while trying to make new relationships—the best advice in the world couldn't change his situation. But Don has faced these challenges without drinking. Recovery does not guarantee a successful life, only the opportunity to succeed.

To me, Don's depression is not as baffling or as troubling as it seems. Addiction is a physical and emotional disorder, and recovery has both physical and emotional components. Even months after Don began recovery, his body was still adjusting to its new life. Depression, unfortunately, is often part of the package. But fortunately, Don—like many others—suffered from a biological depression. His condition is fortunate because Don's depression responded well to a combination of a non-addictive antidepressant and a not-too-demanding exercise program. Given time and a good treatment plan Don found his road to complete recovery.

Don's case illustrates why I believe it is crucial to have *time* in treatment. With time, you have a chance to work out the kinks. The foundation begun with abstinence can take hold, allowing you to place your life in perspective and to systematically build up your personal defenses to fight any threat against your recovery. And to give your body a chance to heal.

Keep your expectations high but be realistic. This chapter presents the physical and mental down side of recovery—not everyone likes to talk about them, but I can almost guarantee that you will experience at least one (and probably more) of the following symptoms or situations. The physical and psychiatric damage that addiction causes may discourage some recovering addicts. But imagine if you had an expensive sports car that you continually drove twenty-four hours a day at 120 mph for ten years straight. Even if the car managed to last ten years, the mechanic's bill would be enormous. That's what long-term addiction does to your body and mind. Your body and mind can be repaired, but it will take time and effort. Being forewarned about the negative aspects of recovery and ready with ways to deal with them will help you confront the down side with more confidence and with more conviction that the pain and struggle is both temporary and defeatable.

The Early Days of Recovery

The first few days of abstinence are the toughest, in one sense, because the addiction is still strong and powerful and you may be physically sick and shaky. If you are in treatment, these days should be easier because everyone in the rehabilitation program is prepared for it and knows what to expect, and your physical and emotional symptoms will occupy your attention to the exclusion of other things. At this stage, you won't have time for wistful thoughts about the good old days.

It's during this initial period that one of the greatest ironies of addiction become clear: most addicts don't take drugs to get high, they take drugs *to feel normal again*. Repeated alcohol and drug use cause the body to alter its production of neurotransmitters, the chemical messengers in the brain that help to regulate our mood and make us feel normal (more information on neurotransmitters may be found on pages 99–107). It's almost as if our brain was lazy, as if it was saying, "Well, why should I bother to produce these neurotransmitters if you're going to give me these drugs?" The greater the drug use, the less neurotransmitters produced by the brain. In essence, the brain "forgets" how to make these chemical messengers. Eventually most addicts (if they live long enough) reach the point where even massive amounts of drugs won't make them feel normal. Then, when the addict first abstains from using drugs, the brain still does not produce enough neurotransmitters. With time, good nutrition, rest, and exercise the supply of neurotransmitters will be replenished naturally, easing withdrawal and renewing health. But while the neurotransmitters are depleted, the brain and the body often combine to create powerful *cravings* that make the addict believe that the only way to feel normal again is to drink or to take drugs. Result: Powerful and painful withdrawal symptoms, which may include mental conditions (such as anxiety, extreme panic attacks, and depression) and physical discomfort (nausea, vomiting, excessive perspiration, etc.).

Withdrawal:
The Necessary ''Evil''

Even the most modern detoxification and withdrawal-management techniques cannot totally eliminate the physical symptoms and emotional upheaval that may accompany abstinence. In most cases, the severity of the withdrawal symptoms depends on how long you have been using and on what chemical had been abused. Certain medications can ease withdrawal, but in most cases I am reluctant to use them: there is often danger of substituting a new dependency for the old. When it's appropriate and safe, however, I will prescribe other medications that can relieve or prevent withdrawal symptoms and are not habituating.

For example, almost all recovering addicts will experience *insomnia* during withdrawal. For most people the insomnia rarely lasts for more than a few days or weeks. Usually a healthy diet combined with a few commonsense strategies, such as reduced caffeine consumption and no caffeine after six P.M. Some people are surprised by the wide range of caffeine-containing products whose consumption must be moderated, from Dr Pepper to Excedrin (see box on page 105 for a list of common caffeine-containing products).

However, for some individuals, most notably heroin addicts or people suffering from major depression, the insomnia may last for months. For these patients I usually recommend evening caffeine abstinence and specific vitamin supplements that access tryptophan from foods (i.e., warm milk, turkey) rich in the amino acid. Mildly sedating and nonaddicting antidepressants such as trazodone (Desyrel) and doxepin (Adapin, Sinequan) are prescribed in more severe cases of drug-induced insomnia. Other amino acids such as tyrosine can help combat mental fatigue and poor concentration. Doctors who are interested in the role of amino acids and cofactor supplementation in the neurochemistry of recovery may want to call 1-800-633-2653, a physician information–referral service that handles questions on this topic.

The following sections chronicle the different withdrawal symptoms associated with each major drug classification.

ALCOHOL

As with other drugs, the severity of alcohol withdrawal varies from individual to individual, the longer someone abuses alcohol, the worse the withdrawal. Unfortunately, alcoholism may take years to develop. Unlike cocaine addiction (which may take only a few months to develop), a person may drink for ten to fifteen years before becoming an alcoholic. After such a long time, the alcohol—and the addiction—has been woven deeply into the fabric of the person's life. And compared to the illegal drugs, alcohol in one way or another has probably been associated with a wider variety of activities: weddings, family dinners, birthday parties, football games, holidays—celebrations of all kinds—have become associated with drinking. It is not an easy pattern to break.

The lengthy time period and ingrained associations of alcoholism increase the difficulty of withdrawal, and no one with a severe drinking problem should try to quit cold on his own. Hospital or inpatient rehabilitation detoxification provides the needed medical attention, including fluids, vitamins, rest, sedation to ease the symptoms, and sometimes other medications to control the potential toxic effects of withdrawal, such as delirium tremens (DTs). DTs is a form of alcoholic psychosis characterized by extreme anxiety, trembling, sweating, upset stomach, and chest pain.

Occasionally, the prescription medication Antabuse (generic name disulfiram) may be used for brief periods to help patients through the withdrawal. Antabuse should only be used to help patients maintain sobriety while receiving other forms of supportive and psychological treatment. Antabuse discourages alcohol consumption by producing extremely unpleasant symptoms whenever the two substances are combined. These symptoms include: nausea, vomiting, shortness of breath, throbbing headaches, chest pain, and blurred vision. Antabuse should only be used under close medical supervision and for a short period of time. By no means is Antabuse a cure for alcoholism—in fact, it is unlikely that the medication *by itself* will have a long-term effect on the drinking patterns of the alcoholic.

COCAINE

Withdrawal runs through several stages. Immediately after using cocaine, the user undergoes a "crash," which begins with a rapid drop in mood, fatigue, and intense craving for cocaine. This craving usually subsides within a few hours, followed by increased fatigue and need for sleep. At this point, people who are not in treatment often use alcohol, antianxiety drugs, sedatives, opiates, or marijuana—just to get some sleep. In treatment, these symptoms can be managed with nutritional supplements, exercise, and the occasional use of nonaddicting, mildly sedating medications, such as the antidepressants trazodone (Desyrel) and doxepin (Sinequan).

Once the cocaine user gets past the acute fatigue and need for sleep, most of the "crash" symptoms disappear. The short- and long-term effects of cocaine usually depend on whether the drug was snorted, smoked, injected, or swallowed (i.e., snorting damages nasal passages, smoking affects the lungs, etc.). Crack, because of the severity and intensity of its abuse, often causes extreme side effects. A 1990 survey of crack users calling the 800-COCAINE hotline found that an alarming 24 percent of the female crack users and 9 percent of the male users had experienced side effects severe enough to require a trip to a hospital's emergency room! The reasons given for these hospital visits included "my heart stopped," "I thought I was going to die," and "my lungs filled up with blood."

A pronounced mental problem in cocaine withdrawal is *anhedonia*—an inability to feel pleasure or enjoyment. Cocaine expert Dr. Frank Gawin of Yale says that the most common complaint of chronic cocaine users is boredom, "since they don't know the word anhedonia." The state can be described as "an empty subjective existence," and during anhedonia the cocaine user may feel the pull toward cocaine-induced euphoria most strongly. This is a major danger period during which many cocaine users return to the old cycle: high–crash–anhedonia–craving–use–high, and so on.

But during treatment, with abstinence and with medical and psychological support, the anhedonia disappears—usually within two to ten weeks. Treatment programs also have the great advantage of protecting the cocaine user against "cues" or reminders of past euphoria that make return to cocaine so tempting during the period of boredom.

Even after the worst is over, there can be moments of intense cocaine craving. Cocaine users seem to have remarkably poor memories of the bad effects of their habit—physical, emotional, and social—and remarkably strong memories of the "highs." The bad memories, which make returning to cocaine less appealing, do seem to return after the craving period is over. Part of treatment is helping you learn to survive the craving and reinforce the reasons you needed to quit.

Compared to cravings for other chemicals, craving for cocaine seems more strongly linked to such influences as your mood, scenes, particular people or events, times of the year, problems with other people, or various objects associated with cocaine use. These associations can be part of the so-called "glamour appeal" of cocaine: fast cars, expensive jewelry, and beautiful people. For the majority of users, these associations are not glamorous: driving past an old nightspot, bumping into the neighborhood dealer, even watching an actor use cocaine in a movie can trigger powerful craving. For this reason, therapy for cocaine dependence deals intensely with techniques to reduce the power of these triggering factors.

MARIJUANA (CANNABIS)

This is not a harmless drug and can produce aftereffects that range from mild to serious. People who use marijuana can suffer loss of energy, memory loss, reduced drive and motivation, apathy, some depression and agitation, and withdrawal from previous interests. These symptoms may persist after marijuana use is stopped. It may be even harder for the cannabis user than for users of other substances to overcome denial, because the drug impairs judgment and prevents the user from gaining any useful insight into his feelings or behavior. However, recovery after abstinence may be quicker than for alcohol or other drugs, with rapid improvement in alertness and mental agility. It's been described as "coming out of a fog."

Other aspects of recovery may be trickier. Since marijuana is so often a young person's drug, therapists have to work to encourage abstinence without severing the user's vital connection to his peers and their culture. If you are a teenage user of marijuana who has decided to quit, you will need to be open minded and patient through this process, to accept the fact that your counselors are not "against" you and your friends but are trying to prevent you from ruining your life with continued drug use. You will be helped to find ways of enhancing your self-esteem, of solving your problems in other ways besides using marijuana, and to discover other, more satisfying and rewarding activities. Your counselors may want to do periodic urine tests during any outpatient rehabilitation. Don't resent it; it is a mark of your success if your tests are negative and a sign to your counselors that you need more help if the tests are positive.

You will be advised to find new friends and stay away from

anybody who uses marijuana or other drugs. This may seem extreme and you may think it's impossible, but the fact is that continued association with pot-smokers is almost guaranteed to make you go back, and continued pot smoking far too often is followed by a switch to heavier drugs.

In treatment, you should be made to feel that someone will be available for you to talk to if you're having unusual stress or if you feel in danger of relapse. The point is to get the support you need in a positive way, and not to seek out drugs or the drug-using crowd for the illusion of support.

Aside from the psychological effects of marijuana, there is physical damage, too, such as bronchitis (usually repaired by not smoking). Incidentally, a joint of marijuana delivers far more potentially carcinogenic "tar" than does a regular cigarette.

Emotional problems associated with marijuana use are complex, affecting your behavior and motivation; they may take as long as a year to resolve.

NARCOTICS (HEROIN, OPIATES, ETC.)

Withdrawal symptoms range from mild craving, anxiety, drug-seeking behavior, yawning, perspiration, runny eyes and nose, restless and broken sleep, and irritability. The eyes may not respond properly to light (i.e., pupils will remain dilated in the presence of bright light). More severe symptoms are muscular twitches, gooseflesh, hot and cold flashes, abdominal cramps, rapid breathing, fast pulse, chills, lack of energy, nausea, vomiting, diarrhea, weight loss, and lack of energy. Not everybody suffers all the symptoms or the most severe ones; the severity of symptoms usually depends on the length and frequency of narcotic abuse. In a hospital, relief during the five to ten days of these symptoms can be provided through various medications (such as clonidone, Methadone, or short-term antianxiety therapy) to ease the physical discomfort and help the user get some sleep. Warm baths, mild exercise, good nutrition, and the compassionate support of physicians, nurses, and counselors also help ease a person through withdrawal. The last item is not the least important.

In the 1960s, Methadone maintenance programs became popular as a means of detoxifying heroin users, and of helping them through withdrawal. Methadone is also addicting, but it doesn't cause sedation. In addition, since it's longer acting than heroin, it relieves addicts of the need for a "fix" every few hours. Therefore, switching to Methadone allows a heroin addict to lead a relatively normal life. Over time, the Methadone dosage is reduced to nothing, thus weaning the addict from all drug use. However, Methadone dependence is notoriously hard to kick.

Long-term recovery for narcotic users, especially heroin addicts, is often made very difficult by malnutrition, sexual infections, and diseases associated with intravenous drug use. These diseases include acquired immune deficiency (AIDS) and hepatitis. In fact, intravenous drug users in many areas of the country are now the group with the highest risk of developing AIDS.

SEDATIVES, HYPNOTICS, ANTIANXIETY DRUGS AND OTHER PRESCRIPTION MEDICATIONS

These can produce severe withdrawal symptoms, including craving, lethargy, insomnia, restlessness, and muscle aches. The quotation from TV news reporter Jim Jenson that opens this chapter attests to the difficulty of prescription-drug withdrawal. In Jensen's case, the medication was Valium (generic name diazepam), a member of a very popular class of medications called benzodiazepines. The popularity of benzodiazepines and benzodiazepine-related agents such as alprazolam

(Xanax), however, has also brought widespread abuse and addiction. Some treatment professionals consider addiction to prescription drugs like benzodiazepines and the other sedatives, such as barbiturates, to be the most difficult to overcome. In fact, *unsupervised, abrupt withdrawal from powerful sedatives can lead to seizures or toxic psychosis and sometimes death.*

Medically supervised withdrawal is a very different thing. The usual strategy is to ease the chemically dependent person through withdrawal with gradually decreasing dosages of whatever drug they were taking. It is usually impossible to reduce withdrawal symptoms so completely that you "don't feel a thing." But the symptoms can be made tolerable, and in treatment you will receive the support you need, along with good advice on exercise and relaxation training, to get you through the bad days.

PSYCHEDELIC DRUGS OR
HALLUCINOGENS (LSD, PCP)

The most common adverse effect of these drugs is the "flashback," which may happen only once after quitting or more often, depending on how often the user took the drug. Flashbacks have been defined as "repeated intrusions of frightening images in spite of all volitional efforts to avoid them." They consist of reliving past drug experiences. The sudden and seemingly unexplainable disruption of present reality can be terrifying. One explanation for these experiences is that the drugs somehow damage the mind's ability to control imagery and fantasy. Another theory suggests that remnants of hallucinogenic drugs remain stored in our body's cells; later, for some reason, these remnants may be released into our bloodstream. Flashbacks usually decrease after a time, but in rare cases can happen as long as a year after the last use of a psychedelic drug. It is not clear whether psychedelic users suffer long-term physical changes in personality (the "acid head" or "acid freak" behavior typical of the 1960s and '70s), or whether these changes simply reflect a change in personal habits and attitudes.

Stopping the use of psychedelic drugs is usually not physically difficult, because they don't produce dependence or craving. But people suffering from psychological symptoms or flashbacks should get appropriate psychotherapy. Occasionally, therapy can be augmented with medication such as buspirone, an antidepressant or antianxiety medication that reportedly does not cause addiction. In any case, as with other addictions, any recovering person who has been addicted to psychedelic drugs must avoid other mood-altering substances.

After Withdrawal: Confronting the Rehab "High"

Many people, immediately after they have made the tremendous decision to get clean and after they have survived withdrawal, feel a tremendous sense of relief, excitement, and accomplishment. This feeling can last for weeks, even months. Some people describe their feeling as like a drug "high" without drugs. You may feel proud of yourself—and with excellent justification. You may feel a tremendous sense of anticipation, of looking forward to life—for the first time in years. While you may want to tell everybody your great news, it may be wiser to postpone wholesale announcements beyond your immediate family. When you have been abstinent for only a short time, many people will be skeptical, and at this stage of your recovery, you don't need any negative signals from anybody. Even your family (or perhaps especially your family) may be skeptical. You may be annoyed and resentful about this, but you can only remind yourself that they have some good reasons to doubt, and to reassure yourself that *you* know you mean it and eventually they will be convinced.

The initial surge of overconfidence and complacency may be short-lived as you begin to realize that early abstinence guarantees no long-term miracles; that you have a lot of learning and growing to do; that abstinence—however rewarding—does not protect you from the ordinary knocks and hard times of life. It is only a phase, a starting place, like early convalescence from illness or surgery. It may hurt until the stitches come out.

But later, when the initial intense physical adjustments seem to quiet down and the addiction appears to be weakened, it's easy to be caught off guard, to begin thinking you could "get by with it" if you took just one drink or one snort.

Some recovering addicts may be surprised to find themselves grieving over the loss of a drug, as powerfully as if a loved one had passed away. Unexpectedly, the times when they were high or stoned take on a new, glamorous sheen—the wild parties, the great sex, the great stories. The memories, however fantastical, make you forget how awful their addiction really was. To someone who is not an addict, grieving for a drug seems strange and incomprehensible. But for most addicts, the drug had become a "loved one," more essential than a wife, husband, parents, or friends. One of our patients at Fair Oaks once remarked: "The first time I tried crack, I knew I wanted to marry this drug. It was what I had been waiting for my entire life." If they're unexpected, the feelings of grief and longing for the times of their drinking or drug taking may surprise some recovering addicts, and lead them back to their addiction.

Dealing with the illusion of the rehab high, and learning to overcome any misbegotten feeling of grief are just two examples of what I like to call the mental "leftovers" of addiction.

The Mental Leftovers
of Addiction

In addition to boredom or anhedonia or cocaine withdrawal, there are several psychological and psychiatric symptoms or conditions that will plague recovering addicts. Many of these problems began with the substance abuse, a few of them may have even preceded the alcohol or drugs—nevertheless, they have persisted into recovery and now must be confronted with all the forces that sobriety can muster.

DENIAL: THE WORD THAT WON'T GO AWAY

Denial is a fundamental and overriding problem in addiction which is still strong during early recovery. Countless times I've spoken with addicts, weeks into their treatment program, who continue to deny the extent of their problem—they're still affected by the "terminal uniqueness" I described in Chapter Two.

If it is beginning to seem as if the word "denial" crops up more often than any other, you are right. Its importance can't be overemphasized, and overcoming denial is essential to success in all the other work you will need to do.

You may feel that because you are abstinent and have taken the first steps toward recovery, you are now in control of your chemical dependence; all you have to do is follow the recovery program until it's time to go and live happily ever after. That is denial of the reality that chemical dependence is a disease that requires long-term vigilance and some fundamental changes in attitude and behavior. You may feel that all your previous problems—with job, home, friends, money—were the cause of your drink or drug problem, and if the people who are helping you will only show you the way to solve those problems, the drinking or drug taking will go away. And you may believe that once that happens, you can drink or take drugs "normally" within acceptable limits, like anyone else. That is denial of the chronic, progressive, physiological nature of substance-dependence disease.

If your treatment program includes attention to psychological problems (which it should as an important and necessary part of rehabilitation) you may feel quite strongly that your substance use was merely a symptom of underlying psychological problems. Until recently, many medical experts would have agreed with this position. However, many treatment professionals, myself included, now believe that while your psychological problems may have led to your taking a drink, these problems did not result in addictive drinking. Although there appears to be a definite relationship between addiction and psychological disorders such as anxiety and depression, *addiction is a disease in its own right*. Millions of depressed or anxious people have taken a drink or used cocaine without becoming addicted. I do believe that some people can become addicted as a result of trying to "self-medicate" their psychiatric problems. But even in this group, the addiction must be treated as a disease along with treatment for the preexisting psychiatric disorders. Similarly, addiction can occur in the absence of any preexisting psychiatric problem, while in itself causing psychiatric symptoms (such as depression; see pages 78–82 for more information).

Believing that your addiction disappeared when the underlying psychological conditions were successfully treated is wrong; *persisting* in this belief is denial. As you work your way through the hard parts of early recovery, and then with good counseling and the support of a group, you will eventually discard all these illusions and recognize that solving your personal problems and gaining insight and new tools for living will help you stay off chemicals, *but only by staying off chemicals can you benefit from this growth*.

THE "I, I, ME, ME" OF GUILT

Guilt is another problem in early recovery. In part, it's natural to feel guilty over all the things you have done to yourself and others. But this differs enormously from acceptance of responsibility.

Guilt provides easy answers, an easy way to duck responsibilities, while tricking the recovering people into thinking they have accepted responsibility and made amends for their past actions. Guilt is, "I'm no good. I'm a rotten human being and nobody likes me, no one loves me, I'm all alone." I, I, me, me. Guilt prevents you from taking responsibility for your actions and for honestly apologizing to the people you have hurt. On the other hand, admitting responsibility and making amends helps not only to repair the damage of your addiction, but it also frees you from feeling guilty. Guilt requires no interaction with other people; it requires no action at all. Responsible action is the antithesis of guilt and the footwork of making amends. Making amends not only repairs damage, it cancels guilt and restores self-esteem. (Actively making amends is necessary to full recovery and is a critical part of twelve-step programs. It is not usually expected in the early recovery period, but this is the time for beginning to recognize guilt as nothing but another form of self-pity.)

Along with guilt goes grief. Grief about lost time, lost love, and irreparable acts. These feelings may be especially acute immediately after you embark on abstinence, as your mind becomes clear again and you have time and opportunity to think and to begin reexamining your life. When you were using drink or drugs, you said and did a lot of things that you may be ashamed of or agonize over now, wishing you could go back and change the past. You will be helped to understand that your past actions were part of your disease and that your present recovery requires total concentration and all-out effort—brooding over the past only detracts from your present recovery.

BAD BEHAVIOR

Everybody who has ever been involved in a treatment program (as a therapist or as a recovering person) learns to recognize certain patterns of behavior, attitudes, and personality types that emerge as a result of the dependence problem and of the challenge of recovering. They have names and catch phrases, which may vary from place to place but which essentially describe the same things. These form an "in" language that serves both as a kind of shorthand communication and as a link that binds the group together, the way medical or legal jargon unites doctors or lawyers. In group therapy sessions and AA meetings, you'll hear statements such as "Poor me, poor me, poor me . . . pour me a drink," or "Run get him his pity pot." To the outside, it may sound odd, but this recovery language can give a person in recovery a strong feeling of belonging, of being united with others who are making the same effort. When you are recovering and you learn to share the symbols, values, and traditions of a treatment group you are better prepared to enter and feel comfortable in a long-term support group such as AA, NA, or CA.

Usually, rebellions and denial—not wanting to feel like part of the recovery group—cover up something else. Arrogance, cockiness, superiority, and aloofness—thinking yourself better than anybody else—are often signs that you don't accept your dependence or recognize that in your dependence (even if not in other ways) you are *exactly* like everybody else who's in recovery. Boredom, or more precisely, the pretense of boredom, may be a way of not taking recovery seriously, of resisting the attempts of others to help you get well. Anyone who works successfully in recovery learns to spot certain behaviors and ways of talking that are a sure indication of resistance. As part of the recovery lingo, they all have names:

The nitpicker: "This is a terrible program. The staff isn't trained. The food is horrible."

The know-it-all: "I don't know why they keep repeating this stuff. It's so obvious. These people don't have anything to teach me."

The independent: "I came here of my own accord, I can leave of my own accord. You can't keep me here."

The gotta-go: "I gotta go clean my house. I gotta go feed my cat, no one knows about her, she hasn't eaten in three days."

The helper: the mother type who focuses on other people's problems; the self-proclaimed counselor who directs attention away from himself by trying to solve everybody else's problems.

The people-pleaser: the one who rushes to help make coffee or clear away chairs after a group session, who compliments and flatters everybody else, who affects modesty and defers to others in a group session "to give them a chance to talk."

One of the remarkable things about group sessions in rehabilitation programs is their ability to cut through the "bull." A group simply will not allow it. Counselors who are themselves recovered or recovering can also be very effective, for the same reasons, but still not as powerfully as a group. In group therapy, when you're sitting with a half-dozen people who've been through what you've been through, and are fighting the same battles you are fighting, confront you with your behavior, it's hard to argue with them or to be resentful or rebellious. Recovering groups are highly sensitive to the attitudes and actions of others in the group, and sometimes stunningly candid about them. This honesty can be a tremendous force in eliciting honesty from those who are still denying, acting, and covering up.

CHANGING MOODS

Regardless of what chemical you were using, in early recovery you will feel many changes of mood and behavior, some of them quite disturbing. This is more likely to happen while withdrawal is still having some effects. Good treatment programs expect these and are structured to deal with them. Nevertheless, it's helpful to be aware of the possibility of such changes and to recognize them as part of a transition to a healthier state rather than as signs of fundamental psychological problems or long-term difficulties.

The boredom or anhedonia of cocaine withdrawal is one of the most noticeable of all these early recovery mood swings. You feel depressed and empty, and this can happen when you stop taking almost any drug. This is partly because you may feel that you have just given up the only thing that for years has provided any pleasure. And when you're not able to feel pleasure, it's difficult to imagine anything that *would* give you pleasure; it's even harder to motivate yourself to try to find something new that will. It's a little like the way you feel right after breaking up a really serious love affair; you can't imagine a person who could make you feel the same, or even imagine that it is possible to fall in love again. In the beginning, you may have to do what AA recommends to people who have trouble believing in a higher power: just start out acting "as if." Pick an activity or make a plan and start doing it *as if* you are going to enjoy it. Try to remember (or ask someone close to you to remember for you) something that you once enjoyed before you became chemically dependent. Nothing may appeal to you at first; the very idea of trying to enjoy yourself may even turn you off. And even when you make yourself do things, you may not feel great pleasure at first. But it will be much better than slumping into a chair and letting depression take over. If you keep at it, you will suddenly surprise yourself by actually having a good time.

To help combat boredom, depression, and anxiety, you need

activity that replaces not only drug taking but all the time-consuming business that goes with it. When you're not occupying yourself most of the day and night with drug seeking, drug taking, recovering from hangovers, trying to scrape money together, time may seem to hang heavy. You may not yet be in physical or emotional condition to engage in anything very demanding such as taking a course in a foreign language or in electronic appliance repair, or any of the satisfying and useful activities you may seek in later recovery. Start simply, with something that can hold your attention while making only minimal emotional demands on you.

Most of all try to recognize that if you are suffering boredom or depression, that's *not* because it is the nature of life in general or of your life in particular. It's not permanent or inevitable. Give it a label: call it anhedonia. That won't make it go away, but it will give you a measure of power over it and it will keep you from succumbing to the feeling that nothing will ever again be as "good" as it was when you were getting high or killing your pain with chemicals.

It is also helpful to learn to recognize and label the kinds of feelings—such as anxiety, depression, discouragement, frustration, or worry—that used to set off cravings and chemical use. You must be aware of the possibility that setbacks in your personal life or work may lead to craving, and that you may not even be aware of why you suddenly feel craving. With help, you can begin to accept these feelings as normal for your situation, to see them for exactly what they are and not confuse them with a need for chemicals. These negative feelings and other setbacks *cannot* be solved by chemicals but can be solved only with the methods ordinary people bring to bear on such problems. Chemical use will only make them worse. Remember, too, that weeks or even months after you stop drinking or taking drugs your body is still making millions of adjustments along the road to its own recovery. Be patient and give your body time to get well, too.

Coping with feelings is made much easier and more useful

in group sessions, which some experts consider the heart of rehabilitation, "a team sport" that loners rarely win. The group provides a safe place for emotional openness about all feelings and thoughts. In the group you learn never to be alone with your painful emotions, but to communicate them so they can be replaced by positive feelings through group support and advice. You will come to learn that the wisdom of a combined peer group is stronger than any one-to-one relationship with a friend, counselor, or therapist. What is especially reassuring is that once you leave a rehabilitation group, the same group support is available for life through twelve-step programs.

However, sometimes the recovering person also suffers from a psychiatric disorder such as depression or anxiety that will not respond to simple patience and support. In these cases of dual diagnosis, treatment by a qualified medical specialist, preferably a psychiatrist, is *essential*. The following sections describe some of the more common psychiatric disorders found in recovery, their relationship to addiction and recovery, as well as their prospects for treatment.

DEPRESSION

Everyone, addicts and nonaddicted "civilians" alike know what it feels like to be depressed. But few civilians—only 6 percent of the general population—experience true, clinical depression. By clinical depression I mean a depression that persists over time (at least a two-week period) and is marked by at least five of the following: fatigue; loss of energy; restlessness; feelings of worthlessness or apathy; impaired concentration, indecisiveness, thoughts of suicide, or changes in appetite, sleep, and/or weight.

But among substance-abusing addicts the incidence of clinical depression is much, much higher than in the general population, perhaps as high as 100 percent in my estimation. As I wrote

earlier, for years experts believed that a psychiatric condition—
depression—caused addiction. Today, addiction is recognized
by many—including myself—as a separate disease. However,
the relationship between addiction and depression is very complex and controversial. Here are just a few of the questions that
a doctor—or a researcher—must ask:

Did the depression cause the substance abuse?

Did the substance abuse lead to the depression?

Is the depression merely a symptom of substance abuse?

Is the substance abuse a symptom of the depression?

The questions go on and on, and it's very easy to get bogged
down and distracted in this debate.

But what I initially tell my patients is far simpler: *Assume you
suffer from both depression and substance abuse.*

As a physician it's my job to discern whether there is a psychiatric disorder such as depression underlying an addiction.
But making the correct diagnosis is impossible if the person
continues to drink or use drugs, so either way an abstinence
period—preferably of at least one month—is necessary before
I can make a diagnosis. There's no way around it: no one can
be treated effectively or perhaps even diagnosed properly, while
still abusing drugs. So if after a "washout" period, the patient
still suffers from depression, I usually prescribe a nonaddicting
antidepressant medication (such as imipramine or desipramine)
to augment the substance-abuse treatment. In many cases the
antidepressant medication does not need to be administered on
a long-term basis. In fact, I have found that as abstinence continues, the incidence of depression declines dramatically. At the
Outpatient Recovery Center, I have estimated that after a one-
year period of abstinence, approximately 12 percent of the recovering patients (roughly double the general population's rate)
require antidepressant therapy. Given enough time, say a few
years of sobriety plus active involvement in AA or other forms
of treatment, this depression rate declines even further, to the
point where it may actually be below the national rate for
depression! I believe this occurs because the recovery process—

when actively applied—is so beneficial and restorative that it has the very positive side effect of combating depression.

ANXIETY DISORDERS

According to a recent survey of over 18,000 people, anxiety disorders were the number one mental health disorder in America, affecting approximately 9 percent of the population. Among addicts the number is much higher: studies of alcoholics in hospitalized treatment programs estimate that from 18 to 32 percent may also be suffering from anxiety disorders. The term *anxiety disorders* actually encompasses several conditions, including, generalized anxiety disorder, panic disorder, phobias, and agoraphobia.

The relationship between substance abuse and anxiety disorders is just as complicated as the relationship between substance abuse and depression. Most experts believe that a significant percentage of individuals repeatedly turn to chemicals, especially depressants like alcohol and tranquilizers, as a means of combating their anxiety, phobias, and panic attacks. The next time you visit the airport, count the number of establishments serving liquor and their close proximity to the gates. It's no accident—bartenders have known for decades that people attempt to quell their fear of flying through alcohol. According to research, the anxiety disorder usually precedes the substance abuse, although other reports suggest that addiction, especially to alcohol and cocaine, may also actually precipitate panic disorder.

Panic Attacks are brief but powerful periods of extreme anxiety characterized by rapid heartbeat, perspiration, chest pain, difficult breathing, and feelings of impending doom. Panic attacks can occur suddenly and for no apparent reason. When these random attacks occur, the person may associate their attack with their current activity or environment—for example, a person who experiences an attack while driving may view driving as the source of their panic. The person then stops driving as an attempt to avoid the panic attacks. A fear followed by this avoidant behavior constitutes a phobia. When the panic disorder is severe, a condition called agoraphobia can occur. (Agoraphobia, commonly called "the fear of the marketplace" is more accurately described as a fear of going beyond a safe area or environment, such as the fear of leaving one's home.)

Many researchers, myself included, believe that there is a strong link between substance abuse and panic disorder. One survey conducted by 800-COCAINE found that 50 percent of the callers reported cocaine-induced panic attacks. Even more disturbing: a recent survey conducted at Fair Oaks Hospital of patients with *no* prior history of panic disorder found that a large percentage of patients experienced panic attacks one month *after* cocaine detoxification! One study found that recovering alcoholics who suffered from panic disorder could not discern the difference between alcoholic withdrawal and a panic attack. Recovering individuals, as Jim Jensen vividly reported in his story about withdrawal, have also reported severe panic attacks during their recovery.

Why does substance abuse lead to panic attacks? One possible theory involves the *kindling* phenomenon. Kindling is thought to occur after areas of the brain are repeatedly stimulated. This stimulation may be caused by the nervous activity of withdrawal (characterized by the "shakes") or by repeated stimulant (such as cocaine) abuse. The stimulation appears to lower the brain's panic threshold—levels of neural activity that had previously been tolerated by the brain will now produce a panic reaction. If these kindled reactions occur frequently enough, the brain's sensitivity may be lowered to the point where little or no activity will cause a spontaneous panic attack.

Panic disorder, when it occurs among the general population, can be treated with a high degree of success—over 90 percent of all patients can be cured by combinations of medications and psychotherapy. Will this impressive success rate hold for panic

patients with a history of addiction? Clinically, I have had success in treating these patients, but will this success apply on a
large-scale level? It's still too early to tell—our understanding
of the complex relationship between panic and addiction is still
evolving—but I am very hopeful that with abstinence and
proper treatment the anxiety disorders can be treated successfully. One thing, however, is indisputable: the millions of people who chose to abuse alcohol, cocaine, and other drugs, *also*
chose to conduct medical experiments on themselves. With recovery, the medical experimentation ceases.

Special Problems among Women: Low Self-Esteem, PMS, and Sexual Abuse

Among recovering addicts, low self-esteem is a formidable op-
ponent. Just when you've begun to put you're life back together
again, just when you've started to feel good about yourself,
some remark or slight will threaten your fragile stability. It may
be an offhand comment from your mother, "You know that
dress really doesn't flatter your figure," or it may be that the
boss forgets to invite you to his party. Whatever the reason,
there's a little voice inside you that's just waiting for the chance
to say, "See, I told you you were no good."

While low self-esteem is a problem among all recovering
addicts, it seems to be especially troublesome among women.
Two specific problems, *premenstrual syndrome* (PMS) and *sexual
abuse*, present special problems for women in recovery.

Studies in the U.S. suggest that as many as 64 percent of all
female alcoholics also have PMS. In some cases women have
even become addicted to the medications prescribed by their
doctors to relieve the PMS symptoms. In recovery, acknowledging, diagnosing, and treating PMS is crucial; without it recovering women are at high risk for relapse.

Women who have experienced the severe anxiety, insomnia,

and mood swings of PMS often learn that nothing relieves the symptoms better than alcohol. Sometimes this leads to alcohol dependence, and it can prevent the alcoholic from achieving or maintaining abstinence if it's not treated properly.

PMS also contributes to the low self-esteem so typical of addiction. One day a woman feels confident and secure in her recovery, then a few days later she is torn by the mood swings of PMS and she feels unable to cope with the sudden changes, changes that she might attribute to recovery. Maintaining abstinence and progressing in recovery become difficult, and she may be accused of not working the Twelve-Steps—of not trying hard enough—by normally well-meaning counselors or friends. These accusations come as the ultimate betrayal and only add to her feelings of failure, compounding her depression.

If you think PMS may be a factor, take note of the onset and duration of your most difficult times in recovery—if they consistently appear around your menstrual period, you should bring this to the attention of your physician or counselor. Making changes in diet and exercise can help—especially avoiding chocolate, salt, and sugar. These can make PMS worse because they increase water retention, which may be a major factor in the headaches, anger, and anxiety of PMS. Unfortunately, they are the things you probably crave most, but if you avoid them, you will usually discover an immediate improvement in your mood and attitude.

Next, sexual abuse.

Until very recently, psychiatry and our society in general have largely ignored the fallout from sexual abuse. But lately, both have become increasingly aware of the problem. The statistics can be staggering: one hospital's survey found that 35 percent of all psychiatric patients had a history of sexual abuse. Another survey of teenagers with a history of sexual abuse found that forty-one percent had been frequent users of marijuana and 24 percent had been frequent users of cocaine, compared to only 5 percent and 1 percent, respectively, of the general teenage population.

In our culture, women have long been silent sufferers—taught to be uncomplaining and self-sacrificing, and to maintain the image of the caretakers whose daily duties, however trying, take no terrible toll. Historically, women have chosen to remain in the shadows rather than face the shame and humiliation that they perceive will occur when their abuse is revealed. In the past, they were often right. But now, for a woman suffering under the dual yoke of a past that includes sexual abuse, and a present diminished by substance abuse, silence only adds to the problem. By not openly confronting the problem, women are made to feel guilty, as if they somehow brought the abuse on themselves. This guilt, in turn, creates a poor self-image.

In a good chemical-dependence rehabilitation program, a woman can feel safe in discussing her most personal experiences. With counseling and especially with group support, she can regain the self-esteem and self-worth she has lost, understand and pursue healthy relationships, respond appropriately to authority figures, clarify personal values, regain spirituality, achieve good physical health, and reach her true human potential.

Special Problems: Adolescents

Sometimes, especially in young people, drug and alcohol abuse lead to a long-term impairment of body and mind called "Post-Drug Impairment Syndrome" (PDIS). If you or a young person you know abuse drugs, the specter of PDIS should be a powerful and frightening warning. It is most likely to follow excessive drug use or to affect people who had psychiatric disease before they started taking drugs. One of the most noticeable symptoms is an inability to endure everyday life stresses and to make a consistent adjustment to society; that is, to hold a job, sustain a marriage, save money, complete school, or even take care of personal belongings such as clothes or a car. People with PDIS may have sudden outbursts of temper, depression, or bizarre behavior, including delusions. According to Dr. Forrest Tennant of the UCLA School of Public Health, people with PDIS often move from house to house or town to town, never staying in one place very long. A young adult with PDIS may stay with parents for a while, suddenly disappear for days, and then return, "completely oblivious to the fact that they left and returned without warning." Some people with PDIS recover or greatly improve if they stay away from drugs for a long time. Sometimes medications help. Sometimes PDIS patients never improve. It is a condition that requires careful diagnosis and treatment, and should be considered if a person who seems to have successfully completed rehabilitation is noticeably disappointed with the results and continues to be troubled by the symptoms mentioned.

The Physical "Leftovers" of Addiction

Addiction is a physical and psychological disease; both preceded and succeeded by physical factors and symptoms. A person's genetic predisposition to addiction is determined long before he or she becomes addicted; and very often a physical backlash also follows addiction. Here's how it works:

Medical research has strong evidence that the physical tendency to become addicted to alcohol is an inherited condition, passed on in families through parents to their children and grandchildren. Most recovering people have a history of addiction in their family. It's estimated that a child with one addicted parent has a thirty-five-times greater risk of addiction when compared to the general public; with two parents addicted, the risk soars to four hundred times greater! A history of alcoholism may be related to an inherited tendency to get hooked on other chemicals: most people entering treatment admit that they used large quantities of drugs and medications to try to patch up or mask physical damage done by alcoholism. Not realizing or wanting to acknowledge that excessive drinking was causing their tiredness, anxiety, aches and pains, weight problems, and insomnia, they went to doctors and came away with tranquilizers, mood elevators, muscle relaxants, pain pills, and sleeping pills. Or they went to "friends" and got cocaine, marijuana, speed, downers, or anything they thought might make them feel good again. Not surprisingly, the result of this alcohol, drug, and medication merry-go-round is further physical damage. As a result, they're in poor health by the time they reach a treatment program.

While the list of physical conditions that result from addiction is formidable, remember that most—if not all—of these disorders can be successfully treated in recovery.

Digestive disorders commonly develop in alcoholics. They include esophagitis (heartburn), vague stomach discomfort, peptic ulcer, acute inflammation of the pancreas, constipation, diarrhea, bloody stools, and stomach cancer. Heavy cocaine use can cause chronic nausea and vomiting. If the drinker or drug abuser succeeds in concealing his addiction from his doctor, he may undergo a lot of expensive medical treatment that doesn't get to the root of the problem.

Alcohol and drug use can cause or contribute to different kinds of **heart disease**. A condition called alcoholic cardiomyopathy diminishes the ability of the heart muscle to pump blood efficiently. The combination of alcohol-induced high blood pressure and heart damage can trigger congestive heart failure. Cocaine constricts the blood vessels and speeds up the heart rate, sometimes tremendously. Marijuana increases the load on

the heart in ways characteristic of stress, causing electrocardi-
ogram abnormalities.

High blood pressure is an immediate effect of both alcohol
and cocaine use, and can also be a long-term effect. After a
single drink, elevations of twenty to thirty points in the systolic
(upper) pressure and of ten to twenty points in the diastolic
(lower) pressure are common. The blood pressure may or may
not drop back to baseline once the effect of the drink wears off;
in some alcoholics who were initially told they had essential
hypertension, blood pressure normalized once they stopped
drinking. With continuing high blood pressure comes an increase in the likelihood of stroke.

Both cocaine and marijuana increase the respiratory rate and
cause **lung damage and other respiratory problems**. Snorted
cocaine dries out the delicate tissues of the nasal passages, causing them to crack and bleed. Continued heavy snorting produces coldlike symptoms with a constantly running nose, or
inflammation of the frontal sinuses accompanied by a persistent
dull headache. Tiny amounts of snorted cocaine that stay in the
nose can eventually erode a hole right through the nasal septum
(the cartilage that separates the nostrils), making plastic surgery
necessary. Long-term cocaine snorting can also damage the vo-
cal cords, causing permanent hoarseness.

Types of **liver damage** that can result from heavy drinking
include alcoholic hepatitis, "fatty liver" (acute infiltration of fat
into the cells of the liver), liver cancer, and the type of cirrhosis
of the liver known as Laennec's cirrhosis. Injecting cocaine or
heroin with a dirty needle can lead to the development of in-
fectious hepatitis.

Since marijuana smokers inhale very deeply and smoke each
joint right down to the end of the butt, marijuana is typically
harder on the lungs than tobacco. A person who smokes both
cigarettes and marijuana doubles the pulmonary insult. In one
study of men who smoked at least one hundred grams of hashish
a month, a third of them developed thick mucus-filled coughs,
wheezing, and breathing difficulties after three or four months.

The Common Cold

The common cold and hay fever pose special problems for people in recovery since a wide range of cold, cough and allergy products—both prescription and nonprescription—contain alcohol, codeine, or other potentially addicting ingredients such as hydrocodone bitartrate and hydromorphone hydrochloride that should be avoided by all recovering addicts. For example, the prescription medication Tussar-2 Cough Syrup contains codeine and alcohol (7 percent of the syrup), while the over-the-counter Nyquil Nighttime Colds Medicine is 25 percent alcohol! Read the ingredients list carefully. I recommend that all preparations containing either alcohol, codeine, hydrocodone or hydromorphone compounds be banned from the house.

This does not condemn the recovering person to a life of constant sneezing and sniffling, however.

Over-the-counter antihistamines are thought not to be addictive. Over-the-counter decongestants often cause sedation or stimulation; it's best to replace them with something very basic and harmless such as a salt-water nasal spray. Cold medications based on aspirin or acetaminophen will not affect mood. Most antibiotics are fine.

For allergy symptoms, your physician may want to prescribe Seldane, which is thought to be nonsedating.

After six to fifteen months, their major ailments were colds, asthma, bronchitis, and sinusitis. Long-term marijuana or hashish smokers, like long-term cigarette smokers, are susceptible to chronic bronchitis and lung cancer.

The **immune system** is vulnerable to alcohol and drug abuse. Heavy drinking can suppress the body's normal production of infection-fighting white blood cells. Unsanitary injection of co-

caine or heroin is widely recognized as a major route of trans-
mission of AIDS.

Brain and nervous system damage are found with all types
of drug abuse. Alcoholics suffer from impaired concentration,
memory, and capacity for abstract thought; blackouts (periods
of amnesia); and hallucinations. Later forms of alcohol-induced
brain damage include seizures, dementia, and the Wernicke-
Korsakoff syndrome (a severe loss of recent-memory capacity).
Both cocaine and heroin can cause death by shutting down the
brain's respiratory control center. Cocaine users are susceptible
to seizures that don't respond to anticonvulsant medications,
and to visual disturbances or hallucinations such as fuzzy vision,
double vision, image distortion, and seeing "snow" (spots of
light in the central vision). In its immediate effects, marijuana
is as dangerous as alcohol in impairing eye–hand coordination
and the ability to drive or operate machinery safely; chronic
marijuana use impairs concentration, memory, and abstract
thinking, similar to those effects seen in alcoholism.

Other physical problems related to alcohol and drug abuse
include *malnutrition, hypersensitivity to light*, and other eye sen-
sitivities; *trauma* (breaks, cuts, bruises, and abrasions from falling); hormonal changes leading to *sexual dysfunction* (diminished
potency or complete lack of desire for sex—see Chapter Seven)
and *disrupted menstrual periods*; and injury to a developing fetus
including *fetal alcohol syndrome* (see box), *congenital cocaine or
heroin addiction*, and *congenital AIDS*.

Fetal Alcohol Syndrome

Pregnant women who drink place an enormous risk upon the lives of their unborn children. Drinking alcoholic beverages of any kind during pregnancy increases the likelihood of offspring developing one or more of the following conditions:

1. Distorted facial appearance

2. Mental retardation or other forms of central nervous system dysfunction
3. Decreased birth weight (prenatal growth deficiency)

Alone, each of the above conditions are classified as *fetal alcohol effects;* when combined they constitute *fetal alcohol syndrome (FAS).*

Even drinking as little as one ounce of alcohol a day has been associated with lower birth weights and spontaneous abortions. The risks of serious fetal side effects increase with the amount and duration of alcohol consumption: women who have three or more drinks a day have three times as many spontaneous abortions as women who consume one daily drink.

Women of a child-bearing age should remember:

1. If you're even considering becoming pregnant, stop drinking now—some studies have found that even drinking before pregnancy occurs has been associated with an increased risk of side effects.

2. If you are pregnant (or even if you think you might be pregnant) and are currently drinking—stop now!

3. All alcoholic beverages—even beer or wine—should be avoided during pregnancy.

4. In general, it's best to avoid all mood-altering substances, including cocaine, marijuana, even caffeine and nicotine during pregnancy. Although no definitive fetal syndromes have been associated with these substances, there remains a strong possibility that their consumption will prove detrimental to the health of the unborn. After all, it took several years of intensive study before FAS could be defined. Using any mood-altering substance during pregnancy is the equivalent of performing a dangerous medical experiment upon the unborn child.

Relieving Pain

Relief of pain during abstinence and recovery can be a special problem for addicts and especially for those whose dependence had been on prescription painkillers. An unfortunately large number of people become addicted to medications that were first prescribed for them by their physicians. If the original source of the pain remains during recovery, or if some new cause of pain arises, it presents a serious dilemma to the dependent and to the physician in the rehabilitation program. In addition, all recovering addicts are at a greater risk for developing any future addiction, including dependence on pain relievers.

Unfortunately, a fear of relapse can lead recovering addicts into many painful and unnecessary situations. For example, a nurse at Fair Oaks hospital had previously entered into a treatment program because of an addiction to pain medication. The nurse recalled how during her recovery from addiction, she forced herself to endure months of pain from several surgical procedures because she was determined never to take painkillers again. This is an extreme and unnecessary predicament; knowledgeable rehabilitation physicians can help relieve pain with nonaddicting or less habituating drugs and with other techniques, such as biofeedback training. This method of learning deep relaxation and control over some nervous-system reactions can be effective, not only for pain but for other symptoms such as anxiety and tension.

At the Outpatient Recovery Center, we've designed procedures for dealing with the most common situations where pain, and pain relief, pose significant problems.

DENTAL PAIN

If you are visiting a dentist for a regular checkup and/or teeth cleaning, no pain relievers or anesthesia are necessary. Potential problems do arise however when cavities must be filled. The local anesthesia used by dentists contains both a numbing agent and a stimulant. Interestingly, the numbing agent—usually Xylocaine—poses no special problems for recovering individuals while providing the main defense against pain. It is the stimulant—normally used to restrict blood vessels and therefore prolong the numbing effect—that poses the greatest risk. However, all dentists should have available a local anesthesia without a stimulant ingredient. Simply inform the dentist that you will need local anesthesia without the stimulant. If you are hesitant to tell the dentist—fearing that your past substance abuse might be revealed—you can tell the dentist that you have high blood pressure. (People with hypertension should avoid these stimulants, since they can raise blood pressure to potentially dangerous levels.) Nitrous oxide—commonly known as laughing gas—is a mind-altering substance and should be avoided. If a root canal or oral surgery must be performed, I encourage my patients to seek either a specialist, or a dentist well-versed in performing the surgery. Often long-term and painful complications (which would require more pain relief than necessary) result from the dentist's inexperience.

If short-term pain medications are needed and if there are no other complications (such as a sensitivity to aspirin), I usually recommend either acetaminophen (Tylenol) or the nonsteroidal anti-inflammatory medications (NSAIDs), such as ibuprofen, piroxicam, and naproxen be prescribed. (See the box below for a list of "safe" pain relievers.)

Non-Addicting Pain Relievers

NONPRESCRIPTION	GENERIC NAME	COMMON BRAND NAMES*
	acetaminophen	Datril, Panadol, Tylenol, etc.
	aspirin	Bayer, Ecotrin, Empirin, etc.
	ibuprofen	Motrin, Nuprin, Rufen
PRESCRIPTION (NSAIDs)	diflunisal	Dolobid
	fenoprofen	Nalfon
	indomethacin	Indocin
	meclofenamate	Meclomen
	mefenamic acid	Ponstel
	naproxen	Naprosyn
	piroxicam	Feldene
	sulindac	Clinoril
	tolmetin	Tolectin

* Space does not allow a complete list of every brand name; for more information please check with your pharmacist or physician.

CHRONIC PAIN

Chronic pain, including back pain and arthritis, often responds well to nonpharmacologic treatments such as exercise, stretching programs, and rest. If pain medications are necessary, I recommend the NSAIDs or aspirin; avoid narcotic pain relievers (such as Tylenol with codeine). When treating muscle or back spasms, some physicians recommend muscle relaxants (such as Flexoril) or even diazepam (Valium). Recovering people should *avoid* these medications; since they can alter mood, the potential dangers outweigh the advantages. The other, nonpharmacologic treatments, such as warm baths, massages, and most importantly, rest, are currently the most effective means of relieving spasms. For the medical treatment of transient headaches (rather than chronic headaches or migraines), I recommend aspirin or acetaminophen; for chronic tension headaches nonpharmacological treatment, including biofeedback, and massage are very effective. For *migraines*, the antihypertensive propranolol (Inderal) has proven to be nonaddictive and effective in preventing the migraine attack.

SURGERY

Obviously, there are times, most often involving surgery and/ or postsurgical recovery, where either anesthesia or narcotic pain relievers cannot be avoided. While it is true that a few recovering individuals do relapse after surgery, the vast majority do not. To minimize the risk of relapsing, I tell my patients to:

1. Prepare mentally for the surgery by increasing their participation in a twelve-step program. Tell your sponsor and close friends of the impending risk, and welcome their support in helping you through this period.

2. Tell your doctor of your addiction and ask that your medications be kept to minimum. For example, ask her to prescribe

only a single day's dosage—with no refills. This means that you will not be able to take more than your prescribed daily dose at one time; unfortunately it also means that you must call your doctor for a new prescription for each day that it is necessary. However, this reduces the temptation to exceed your dosage, while allowing the physician to carefully monitor your medications. Most physicians will understand your reasons for requesting this prescription pattern (if they don't, you should look for another doctor).

Regrettably some recovering alcoholics and drug addicts develop a *cross-tolerance* to pain medication. Just as these people developed a tolerance to a specific drug (alcohol or cocaine) and then needed an ever increasing amount of drugs to achieve the same "high," some recovering patients will need higher than normal amounts of a painkiller or anesthetic to achieve the same relief. If this is the case, I strongly recommend that participation in support groups be increased both prior to and after the surgery.

After reading about the down side of recovery, it's time for some good news . . .

4

HELP FOR THE BODY AND THE MIND

WHEN CONFRONTING ALL OF THE PSYCHOLOGICAL AND PHYS-
ical issues of recovery, you must remember that you can also
strike out in other constructive directions: exploring new, enjoyable ways to take care of yourself and regain your lost health
and fitness.

A word of caution: since you know you're vulnerable to
compulsive alcohol or drug use, you're likely to be vulnerable
to compulsive dieting and exercising, too. Try to avoid ex-
tremes, though: for example, one person who attended the Fair
Oaks outpatient program, subsequently decided to lose weight,
and became so obsessive about dieting that she would "atone"
for a piece of cheesecake by eating nothing at all for two days
afterward. Another patient, a recovering cocaine addict, who
took up jogging with such single-minded intensity that if for
any reason he failed to run his daily five miles he considered
the day ruined. "Overachievement" of this kind is *not* part of
a healthy recovery. You're aiming for serenity, moderation,
common sense, and enjoyment of life—not heroics.

DIET

At the beginning of your recovery period, you may be grappling with one or more of the following diet-related problems:

Overweight: Weight problems are a source of concern and unhappiness to the majority of people in recovery, and it's easy to see why. Calorically speaking, alcohol, a concentrated carbohydrate, is one of the world's richest "foods." A single ounce of alcohol supplies seventy calories—as much as an egg or twelve almonds. That's why people who drink heavily often put on weight, even if they're not big eaters.

Delta-9-tetrahydrocannabinol (THC), the main psychoactive component of marijuana, leads to weight gain by encouraging the body's salt retention. Also, many users of marijuana and hashish gain weight from frequent "stoned" binges on foods high in sugar, salt, and fat, such as cream-filled cakes and cookies, potato chips, and corn chips.

If you're unhappy about being overweight, recovery will offer you a unique opportunity to make some permanent, wholesome, and "slimming" changes in your eating habits.

Underweight: Anyone who has waged a lifelong battle-of-the-bulge may find it hard to believe that severely underweight people aren't in good condition, but it's true nonetheless. You may be among the minority of people in recovery who actually need to gain weight in order to feel better. Long-term alcohol abuse can cause stomach pain, vomiting, and diarrhea, and can aggravate peptic ulcers. If you were a drinker, gastrointestinal distress may have caused you to avoid food and lose weight despite the calories you drank.

Cocaine and crack, unlike alcohol, provide no calories whatsoever and suppress the appetite. If you wasted away while you were dependent on either of these drugs, it's no wonder—you were literally starving yourself.

Malnutrition: Not only does drug-induced appetite loss lead to undernourishment, but in addition, alcohol itself contributes to malnutrition. Although alcohol is a high-calorie item, the calories are empty—they supply almost no protein components, vitamins, or minerals. This means that if you got two-thirds of your daily calories from alcohol, as many alcoholics do, you may be overweight and malnourished at the same time. Alcohol has rightly been called not a nutrient, but an "antinutrient." Incidentally, it's a myth that beer and wine are vitamin-rich. Just as an example, you'd need forty quarts of beer or two hundred quarts of wine to meet your daily requirement for vitamin B-1.

"Sugar Swings": Food has a definite effect on mood. High quality protein foods from meats, dairy products, and complex carbohydrates such as grains and legumes (kidney beans, chick peas, and lentils) stabilize your blood sugar level and help sustain a feeling of well-being. At the opposite extreme, refined or simple carbohydrates, such as ordinary white sugar, can contribute to depression, lack of energy, and unhealthy food or drug cravings.

Why does blood sugar affect our mood? To function smoothly, your body needs a steady supply of a simple sugar, called glucose, in the blood. The food you eat gets digested and broken down into glucose. Alcohol, and also "junk foods" that are high in refined sugar, cause the level of blood glucose to shoot up abnormally high. The pancreas responds by pumping out a large quantity of insulin to break down the sugar. The insulin that's left over causes blood glucose levels to drop too low again. At this point, your heart and muscle performance weaken, your brain and nervous system work below par, your energy level and endurance drop, and you feel emotionally shaky and vulnerable. You reach for another high-sugar junk food item, or a quick pick-me-up such as coffee, alcohol, or cocaine. Once again, the pancreas overreacts with an excessive spurt of insulin, and the circle continues.

Neurotransmitter Imbalance: The messages that travel between brain and nerve cells are carried by chemical messengers called neurotransmitters. Your brain constantly uses certain amino acids—building blocks derived from the proteins you eat—to form various neurotransmitters in the right amounts. But alcohol and drug abuse disturbs the neurotransmitter balance in two ways: by interfering with good nutrition, thus cutting down on your body's supply of available amino-acid building blocks; and by "sabotaging" your brain cells, fooling them into slowing down their production of certain neurotransmitters.

With your brain and nervous system thus thrown out of whack, you suffer from depression, anxiety, and insomnia. These effects continue for at least a month after you stop drinking or using drugs, while your injured cells gradually repair themselves.

These are the three neurotransmitters that alcohol and drug abuse are known to deplete: *dopamine* and *norepinephrine*, which activate the body and promote alertness and energy; and *serotonin*, which quiets the body and promotes calmness and sound sleep. Although alcohol, marijuana, and other chemicals are all thought to deplete the body's supplies of neurotransmitters, cocaine is particularly notorious for eroding supplies of dopamine. As we'll see shortly, good nutrition and, in some cases, amino acid and vitamin supplements can help speed your recovery of healthy neurotransmitter production and activity.

Chaotic eating habits: Now that you're sober, you're working on getting your life back together. But you're behind on the mortgage, your bills and paperwork are backed up, you have a new job, you're trying to pay more attention to the people in your life—it's hectic. Who has time to eat breakfast? Who has time to shop for fresh foods, let alone cook them, not to mention washing the dishes afterward?

Eating out all the time isn't the answer. Restaurant food is generally high in salt, saturated fat, and sugar—just what you don't need. Somehow, you'll need to find time to eat right.

When you're still in the stage of white-knuckle sobriety, you'll find yourself repeatedly craving the temporary "high" you can

Neurotransmitters and Nutrition

Neurotransmitter	Depleted in alcohol abuse	Depleted in cocaine abuse	Effect of depletion on mood	Amino-acid building block	Occurs naturally in
Dopamine, Norepinephrine	X	X	No energy or drive; poor concentration; depression	Tyrosine	Protein-rich foods: eggs, fish, meat, etc.
Serotonin	X	X	Agitation; inability to tolerate delay; insomnia	Tryptophan	Warm milk with honey; turkey

Regular meals that include lean, high-quality protein provide the amino acids necessary to rebuild depleted supplies of dopamine, norepinephrine, and serotonin. Amino acid supplements may speed the rebuilding process.

get from high-calorie sweet and salty foods such as donuts, ice cream, and potato chips. You won't have to look far, because junk food is everywhere.

Junk foods can set off a roller coaster of blood sugar highs and lows. Because of this, they have a peculiar power to bring out compulsive behavior. The classic case is the guy who gets out of bed at midnight, starts up the car, and runs down to the convenience store for an ice cream "fix." You just don't see that kind of craving for Brussels sprouts.

Another factor contributes to your strong desire for sweets. Addiction so overwhelms the body that it prevents us from experiencing the pleasures of food. In recovery, your long-denied taste sensations blossom again—food tastes good again and your body often turns to eating with a vengeance.

As a physician, I know the problems associated with excessive weight gain and I would certainly like all of my patients to maintain their weight at a healthy level throughout their recovery. But as treatment provider, I am even more aware of the very real dangers of relapse. While I do certainly not encourage these sugar binges, I tell them that they must use whatever it takes to avoid relapse. Later, after their recovery has returned them to a more stable state, I'll suggest a double strategy for coping with junk food cravings: (a) eat frequent small meals of fresh foods and lean proteins—this prevents blood glucose "lows"; and (b) substitute fruit for high-sugar sweets. Fruit sugar ultimately satisfies your sweet tooth better. You might eat a dozen donuts at a sitting, but would you eat a dozen peaches?

What about caffeine addiction? According to the old joke, all you need to do to find the nearest AA meeting is follow the Maxwell House delivery truck. Early recovery is a time when you're apt to go on coffee binges. Why? Because the caffeine in coffee draws forth a rush of energy and alertness—just what you're longing for if drinking or drug use has depleted your stores of the "wake-up" neurotransmitters, dopamine and norepinephrine.

But heavy coffee drinking is a short-sighted remedy for the blahs. The caffeine high, like the sugar high, is followed by a letdown—a low period of fatigue and diminished energy. This makes you want more coffee, and you're off and running on another circle of highs and lows. Furthermore, excessive caffeine contributes to insomnia, a common problem among recovering addicts. We usually associate caffeine with coffee, but caffeine actually shows up in a wide range of products.

People differ in their sensitivity to caffeine. If you're not particularly affected by it, go ahead and have one or two cups of coffee a day. But if regular coffee and caffeine revs you up and then lets you down, you'd better stick to caffeine-free products and avoid the products listed on page 105.

If you are consuming over five hundred milligrams of caffeine each day and you wish to reduce this amount, I suggest that you cut back gradually over a two-week period. Abruptly ceasing your caffeine consumption can cause withdrawal symptoms, including headache, severe fatigue, and drowsiness.

It's particularly important to boost your protein intake in the early weeks and months of recovery, even if that means eating more meat and animal products than you're used to. If you're trying to lose weight, if you have trouble digesting fats, or if your doctor has told you to cut down on cholesterol, you should go easy on animal fats—marbled steaks, bacon, sausage, eggs, cheeseburgers, butter, cream, whole milk, and ice cream. Instead, reach for lean meats, tub margarine, skim or 1-percent milk, and lowfat yogurt. It's also important to know that certain combinations of vegetable proteins from complex carbohydrates found in grains and legumes (kidney beans, chick peas, and lentils) provide protein that's just as high quality as the protein in meat. To learn more about this, consult *Diet for a Small Planet* by Frances Moore Lappé and *Recipes for a Small Planet* by Ellen Buchman Ewald.

Besides making sure your total protein intake is adequate, you should concentrate on getting a fair portion of that protein in the morning. Eating protein for breakfast is important to

---

Nutritional Aftercare:
The Sobriety Diet

I have a few basic recommendations for your nutritional aftercare program.

To balance your diet, make sure you eat something from each of these basic food groups every day. Ideally, a meal should include something from all three groups:

Vegetables and Fruits: Asparagus, beans, broccoli, carrots, celery, corn, cucumbers, lettuce, onions, peas, peppers, squash, tomatoes, apples, apricots, bananas, berries, cherries, grapefruit, grapes, melon, mango, nectarines, oranges, peaches, pears, pineapple, plums.

Protein: Beef, cheese, chicken, cottage cheese, eggs, fish, pork, tofu, turkey, milk, veal, yogurt.

Starches: Brown rice, brown bread, pasta, potatoes, whole grain cold cereals, oatmeal, whole-wheat crackers.

---

give you energy and stamina for the day, and to avoid that midmorning moment of starvation that starts you thinking about pastries—or a drink, or a hit of cocaine.

However, you may feel that you can never eat much in the morning without feeling sick. Up till now, your idea of a good breakfast may have been a caffeine-and-sugar jolt of black coffee and a danish. This is just what you want to avoid—a rush, followed by a crash. But if the very thought of eggs and Canadian bacon in the morning makes you gag, you'll need a special strategy. To get started, try one of these light but nourishing breakfasts, and follow up with fruit or toast as a midmorning snack:

Light Breakfast 1: Shredded wheat with blueberries and lowfat milk.

Common Sources of Caffeine

Product		Caffeine
Instant coffee	1 cup	66 milligrams (mg)
Coffee—percolated	1 cup	110 mg
Coffee—drip brewed	1 cup	146 mg
Tea—brewed 1 minute	1 cup	25 mg
Tea—brewed 5 minutes	1 cup	46 mg
Cocoa	1 cup	13 mg
Jolt Cola	12-ounce can	120 mg
Coca-Cola	12-ounce can	60 mg
Dr Pepper	12-ounce can	60 mg
Tab	12-ounce can	49 mg
Pepsi Cola	12-ounce can	43 mg
Chocolate bar	approx. 2 ounces	25 mg

Nonprescription stimulants:

Vivarin	200 mg
Caffedrine	200 mg
No Doz	100 mg
Pre-mens Forte	100 mg
Aqua-Ban (over-the-counter diuretic)	100 mg

Nonprescription medications:

Excedrin	64 mg
Vanquish	32 mg
Anacin	32 mg
Emprin	32 mg
Midol	32 mg
Dristan	16 mg

Reprinted with permission from *Overcoming Insomnia*, by Donald R. Sweeney,
M.D. (New York: G. P. Putnam's Sons. 1987).

Light Breakfast 2: Boiled or scrambled egg, rye toast, a quarter of a canteloupe.

Light Breakfast 3: Orange or pineapple juice, thin slices of sharp cheddar cheese on whole-wheat toast.

Eventually, your tolerance for breakfast may increase to the point where you can have a substantial, protein-rich morning meal every day. You'll be amazed at how much better you feel throughout the day.

An old adage advises us to eat like kings in the morning, princes at noon, and paupers in the evening. If you're faithful about getting a good high-protein breakfast, you can follow this advice with no problem. There's no need to stuff yourself at dinnertime if you've eaten well earlier in the day. You'll sleep better, and shed excess pounds faster, if you go easy on dinner.

If eating three meals a day is terrific, eating six is even better. Six meals? Yes, six mini-meals of healthful foods—or three modest meals and three light snacks—will be even more effective at keeping your blood sugar and neurotransmitter levels in line. This technique is well known among insulin-dependent diabetics, some of whom are skilled at using frequent wholesome snacks to keep their blood sugar within tight margins. If you're planning a day at the mall or a long trip by car, pack a sandwich and a supply of snacks such as apples, peanuts and raisins, and fruit juice or mineral water, so that intense hunger won't force you to resort to coffee-shop or fast-food fare.

How about vitamin pills and other supplements? In early recovery, a daily multivitamin-and-mineral tablet is usually a good idea, since virtually all kinds of substance abuse deplete the body's stores of the B-complex vitamins, vitamin C, and various trace elements. Check with your doctor to make sure you've chosen a safe vitamin formulation; certain vitamins, notably A and D, can be toxic in large dosages.

Besides taking vitamins, you may want to ask your physician about supplementing your diet with amino acids, such as tyrosine, that help produce neurotransmitters. I must stress the importance of checking with your physician first: the Food and

Drug Administration has reported numerous cases of a rare blood disorder linked to excessive l-tryptophan consumption; and has banned over-the-counter sale of tryptophan.

I usually recommend taking the *tyrosine* tablet in the morning on an empty stomach. Half an hour later, eat a breakfast that includes high-quality protein, such as an egg or lowfat cheese. This will boost your production of the two "energizing" neurotransmitters, dopamine and norepinephrine.

To help get a good night's sleep, I usually suggest avoiding caffeine in the evening, taking supplements that promote dietary trytophan, and drinking milk or eating a slightly sweet snack, but *no protein* at bedtime.

Some patients and staff members at Fair Oaks like to buy amino acid–containing tablets that also include certain B-vitamins and minerals. The extra ingredients are said to help transport the amino acids to the brain, where they are transformed into neurotransmitters.

If your physician recommends amino acid supplements in early recovery, you should continue them for a month or two (again with the approval of your physician). Then, if you're eating regular, nutritious meals, avoiding junk food, and feeling good, you may not need the supplements any more.

Making time for meals takes planning, especially for habitual meal skippers. If you find your mornings are always too rushed to allow for breakfast, try setting the alarm clock twenty minutes earlier.

Exercise: Reliable Road to a Natural High

In your search for a comfortable, enjoyable sobriety, exercise and diet are natural allies.

First, let's deal with the question of medical supervision. Although people are always told to seek medical advice before they exercise, most don't believe that's really necessary. For you, though, it's different. Because you're emerging from a chemical dependence that has weakened several organ systems within your body, checking beforehand with your doctor is critically important. You may have unsuspected liver, heart, or circulatory problems, high blood pressure, anemia, or some other condition that could spell trouble if you overexert yourself suddenly. Make sure your doctor knows your history of chemical dependence, and ask him what short-term and long-term goals are realistic for you.

That said, there's nothing as wonderful for your body and spirit as a regular program of aerobic exercise.

Aerobic—you've heard it often enough, but what does it really mean? It simply describes sustained, rhythmic exercise in which your body uses oxygen to help meet its fuel demands. Examples of aerobic exercise are fast walking, jogging, swimming, jumping rope, and riding a bike or an exercycle.

To benefit fully from aerobic exercise, you should do it steadily for fifteen or twenty minutes at a stretch. Your heart will be beating faster than usual, but not pounding madly. Aim to exercise at a level comfortable enough that you can simultaneously carry on a conversation.

Another warning: as a novice, the biggest mistake you can make is to set yourself an unrealistic exercise goal at the outset. Even if you broke speed records as a runner on the high school track team fifteen years ago, don't expect to perform at that level now! If you push yourself too hard and end up sore and exhausted, you're liable to give up right away. Start gently and work up very gradually.

Begin with a *warm-up* exercise. Use the same motions required by the exercise you're planning to do, but do them in slow motion. Be sure to start out with a warm-up every time you exercise, to prime your body for the effort it's about to make.

After you've worked out for fifteen or twenty minutes, give yourself a *cool-down* at the end of the exercise period. The cool-down is vitally important because it helps your body make a smooth transition from stress back to a normal state. Taper off during the last few minutes of your exercise, to bring your circulation back to baseline. If you've been cycling hard and you fail to cool down, your leg muscles will contract, trapping blood and preventing it from continuing on its normal route to the brain. This can make you feel light-headed and dizzy.

As you move further along on the road to recovery, you'll grow increasingly aware of the intimate connection between mind, body, and spirit. Regular aerobic exercise—three times a week, or ultimately even once a day—is more than a physical boost and a mental stimulant. By redirecting the energy you used to spend on alcohol or drugs, exercise also helps you to explore your own spiritual dimension.

As you slowly allow your physical talents to unfold, you develop a relationship with what's *outside* you: the road or track if you're running, for example, or the water if you're swimming. When you hit stride and reach your comfort zone, you feel at one with your exercise and with the world. At this point you've attained what's rightly called a "natural high," caused by *endorphins*—the body's natural opiates, produced by the brain itself. Unlike an artificial chemical euphoria, this natural high is good for you. You're not just exercising any more; you're celebrating life. It's wishful thinking to suppose that good diet and regular exercise are all it takes to overcome an addiction. Diet and exercise are only adjuncts to your decision to stay sober, assume responsibility, and participate actively in a support group. But they're pleasurable adjuncts! They'll help transform your white-knuckle sobriety into the true joy of living.

Recovery Takes Time

In the first week or two of treatment, most chemically dependent people are physically and emotionally unable to achieve the kind of "surrender to the treatment process" that was described in Chapter One. It takes time for the brain to heal, for the recovering person to relax, make friends, and open up to strangers. All members of twelve-step groups recognize the pattern of behavior of the newcomer who sits in the very back row, leaves the minute the meeting is over while others are talking and socializing, and never volunteers to speak. It takes time for the newcomer to move up to the front row, where he is most likely to be invited to "share" by talking about himself.

You may be afraid to trust strangers with your future, or you may be unwilling (usually subconsciously) to admit that you are an alcoholic or addict. Such a label is frightening, and you probably feel that you don't deserve it and certainly don't want it; all you want is to be "normal" like everyone else. You may also feel angry about these things. This is also understandable, but must be recognized and expressed; studies of recovering chemical dependents have shown clearly that anger gets in the way of recovery only if it is internalized, or buried and left unexpressed.

You have had a life-threatening disease that went on for a long time; give your body and your mind equal time to recover. Keep a journal, so you can look at your progress over a period of time—but don't compare every day with the day just before. Be proud of any progress. Don't despair when things seem to slide backward; recovery is not a straight line upward but a series of curves and dips. Don't look at yesterday—look farther back to the time when you were "out there," and then you will see how far you've come. It is also helpful to realize that much of your moodiness and negative feelings are related to nervous system damage and to the withdrawal syndrome. With medical attention, good nutrition, and exercise, these uncomfortable feelings will ease, and you will feel as if you have been reborn.

But even in these "glory days" of recovery, the danger of relapse will *always* exist . . .

5
RELAPSE AND RELAPSE
AVOIDANCE

WHY WOULD ANY RELATIVELY SANE HUMAN BEING WHO HAS been through the hell of chemical dependence, and has begun to live a real life and to feel well and decent again, want to go back again?

Why would anyone who has struggled so hard to get off drugs or drink, who has recognized that drugs or drink are a death sentence, ever want to touch the stuff again?

There is a scene in a television movie about Bill W., the founder of Alcoholics Anonymous, in which he stands looking out of a window with his back to his wife and speaks passionately to her about his alcoholism and his most recent of many attempts to remain sober. He talks of his shame and guilt, of the pain he feels over the harm he has done to her, of his intense wish to remain free of drink and lead a decent life. Then he turns to her and says very slowly and with agony in his voice: "But what I want most in all the world right now . . . is a drink."

Ask any recovering alcoholic or drug user and he will probably tell you that he desperately wants not to drink or to take

111

drugs but to fashion a new life, one worth living. But go to any twelve-step meeting and you will hear at least one person during the hour who is trying to recover for the second or third time.

Nobody wants to relapse. Few people plan to do it. Some people have no idea why they did it. The fact is that chemical dependence is an illness that can be defined by its propensity to relapse. And just as there's no such thing as being "a little bit pregnant," there's practically no such thing as having just a "little slip." In rare cases a person may relapse on one occasion and then immediately get back into treatment or a group. But for the most part, chemically dependent people can't have "just one" without being in danger of having another, and another, and another . . .

That is why, although no individual is destined to relapse, every chemically dependent person must know the danger, prepare for it, try to prevent it, and deal with it if it happens.

Why Relapse?

There are many reasons for the tendency toward relapse. It is generally agreed that people with a physiologically and genetically based *susceptibility* or allergy to drink and drugs never lose that susceptibility. When they drink or take drugs, they have a physiological reaction that is different from other people's, that feeds and perpetuates the craving for drink or drugs.

That is the simplest and most obvious explanation for the fact that one drink or one dose can mean disaster. It doesn't explain why anyone who knows the danger would take that one drink or dose in the first place. There are, in fact, many reasons and many motivations. Some people who appear to have successfully recovered may still find it difficult—even a long time after their last drink or drug—to accept "never again." People resent and resist being barred forever from things that other people are able to enjoy with impunity. They cannot conquer the yearning to be like other people, to be able to drink socially or use drugs "recreationally." Even if they know they shouldn't and can't, the instinct to deny the illness and the wish to be able to try it and get away with it are almost irresistible. It is incredible but true that diabetics, whose lives may be dramatically and immediately threatened by sugar, sometimes go on candy or cake binges.

Another reason for relapse is that addicts have become so dependent on drink or drug to relieve pain or tension or even mild discomfort that such things automatically trigger the habitual response of reaching for a glass or a pill or a line. Chemically dependent people are often highly susceptible to "cues" that subconsciously stimulate the desire for the chemical. Still another reason is social pressure; it can be very difficult in our society to be the only abstainer. (This "excuse" is weakened by the fact that drugs are still not so ubiquitous that one is constantly required to say no, and the increasing popularity of nonalcoholic drinks at parties means the recovering alcoholic doesn't stand out like a black fly in a glass of milk.)

Another element is what's called *reinforcement*. Drinking or taking drugs has been described, accurately I think, as "behavior maintained by its consequences." If the consequences are good, they reinforce and thus maintain the behavior. This is true of drink and drugs because their immediate consequences are good—although the long-term results are lethal. Drugs and alcohol, for instance, have the good effect of ending such unwelcome states as pain, anger, anxiety, or depression, which makes the user repeat the behavior whenever these states arise. Drinking and using drugs are also reinforced if this behavior wins the approval of friends or conveys a special status. Short-acting drugs, such as cocaine and some barbiturates, are particularly strong perpetuators of habitual use because they can cause such reinforcement several times a day, day after day. Even the paraphernalia associated with drug use become reinforcers.

Most relapses happen within the first few months after being discharged from inpatient treatment or after entering some other form of therapy or group support. So now you're abstinent. What have you got? Initially, not much more than loneliness, fear, guilt, resentment, and broken relationships. At a follow-up visit a week after his discharge from Fair Oaks, Don admitted things weren't going well: "Today my wife left me, my daughter went with her, I found out I'm losing the car. I'm starting to think, 'If this is sobriety, is it worth it?' " Don had the beginning of recovery, but only the beginning: a newly acquired habit of nondrinking and nondrugging which was not yet strong enough to operate automatically; a new perspective on himself which hadn't had time to penetrate deeply into his thinking and behavior; and a lot of repair work to be done at home, on the job, and with his friends. What he didn't have was his old friend, the bottle: the escape, the pain killer, the pleasure giver.

Like all human beings, you are exposed to and are bound to suffer from the "wear and tear" emotions of anger, frustration, and resentment. Most recovering drinkers and drug takers will testify that it is not the big things, like tragedy, grief, job loss, or broken romances that get you so much as the piling up of a million daily stresses and suppressed emotions. That's why it's not surprising that relapse, which is fairly common in early recovery, can still happen even much later.

The Rules of Relapse

The two important rules are these:

First, use *all* of your energy and determination, *one day* or even *one hour* at a time, to avoid a slip.

Second, *plan ahead* for hazards and temptations.

Arlette had completed rehab and wanted to visit her parents, whom she hadn't seen since she had stopped drinking. She was proud of her recovery and expected that her parents would be supportive and happy. She was so confident about this that she neglected to think ahead and make plans about the dangers of the visit. Her parents *were* proud—but while she had been changing, they had not. During the visit, her father was "picky" and made slighting remarks that undermined her self-esteem. Her compulsively neat mother was in a constant state of tension and worry that Arlette's four-year-old son was about to break a crystal vase or spill his juice on the carpet. Both parents were wary and suspicious; they seemed to be watching Arlette's every move as if at any moment she might go off and sneak a drink. Not surprisingly, before the weekend was over, she did.

Arlette still needed to develop a repertoire of important relapse-preventing strategies. For instance, she could have reminded herself that her parents' tense behavior reflected *their* problems with her drinking past, not *her* present failures or shortcomings. Second, she could have spoken directly with her parents, explaining that she had not fully recovered, that relapse was always a danger, and that she could cope better if she had their understanding and encouragement. They might have acted differently if they had known that their vigilance made her more likely to slip, not less.

There are thousands of variations on the theme of planning ahead. A patient of mine named Patrick had a son who was about to be married. Patrick longed to celebrate the day, and stay up half the night to party with everyone else. The morning of the wedding, he spent an hour or so talking to his AA sponsor. At the reception, he allied himself with a cousin who had been in recovery for several years, stayed by him as much as possible, and sought him out when he was feeling especially uncomfortable. He drank a lot of ginger ale and got through the day not "one day at a time," but literally "one hour at a time."

In one sense, chemical dependence is a disease much like arthritis: it can be treated, and the symptoms can be greatly relieved, but it has a tendency to flare up again. However, you can take steps to reduce the likelihood of recurrence of your chemical dependence. And even though a slip is serious, you can't use it as an excuse to give up entirely. Relapse is a learning experience, not a total defeat. If it happens, take the time to figure out the reason for the relapse. That way you can take extra precautions against that particular danger or temptation, or work harder on that aspect of recovery.

Sometimes, unfortunately, it almost seems as if something in you doesn't *want* to stay recovered. Part of that "something" is the biochemical defect or deficiency that contributes to dependence. Part of it may be counterproductive eating habits, as we saw in the previous chapter—a tendency to binge on sugary foods, and thus to swing frequently from high energy to fatigue and depression. In early recovery, there has not been enough time or nutritional correction to diminish your urge for a quick fix.

Emotional and psychological factors also play a big role. One of them is the almost irresistible impulse to find out things and to experiment. Human beings are by their nature curious; it is one of their most noticeable characteristics and one of their best. It leads to learning, discovery, art, music, invention, exploration. A small child may be told that he is not yet old enough to climb a particular tree, but might try to climb it anyway. Perhaps he'll make it without a spill, perhaps he'll fall and even hurt himself. But chances are, he's likely to try again. He can't accept the limitation; he thinks he must have simply made some error in the way he climbed it the first time; he may also have the small child's innocent confidence that he can do anything— even if he's just proved he couldn't. Chemically dependent people are much like that. Some people deliberately seek out old drug-taking friends or visit their favorite bar just to see how they will feel or test themselves to prove they are strong enough to resist temptation. Dr. Mark Gold has said that a user who tries this is "orchestrating his own relapse."

Reinforcing this urge to experiment or test is the persistent notion that it is possible to "control" drinking or drug taking once the worst of the dependence has been overcome. People who have been heavy drinkers or drug users who were almost perpetually drunk or stoned get the mistaken idea that this is the definition of drinking or drug taking, and that "a little bit once in a while" is not at all the same sort of thing.

What they have not yet faced is the reality that for the chemically dependent, *there is no such thing as a little bit once in a while.*

Why does "just one drink" almost always lead to more? One drink or one dose of a drug sets up a whole constellation of effects. First, it reminds you (both consciously and physiologically) of the high or the relaxation or the relief of pain you always got with more than one. Yet one doesn't achieve that effect. It's a disappointment, a mere shadow of the former effect, just enough to remind you but not enough to really do anything for you. You have to have another to get the real effect. Furthermore, that one also triggers a reminder of the withdrawal effects you used to get after you had more than one—and you have to have another to kill the withdrawal effects.

Finally, and most important, is the fact that as soon as you take one, you begin to lose the discipline and conscious control you have over chemicals when your mind is clear and free of chemical influence. Whatever skills you may have learned in maintaining abstinence are suddenly rendered useless; you can't apply them when you need them most, because the one drink or one drug erases them from your mind and strips you of the power to apply them.

It's best not to be swayed by a few studies that claim some recovered alcoholics or drug addicts can return to occasional "social" drinking or drug taking. These studies involved intensive training and a strictly controlled environment. In fact, the number of successful "controlled users" is microscopic compared to the number of people who have failed and even died trying. It's mostly wishful thinking that perpetuates the myth of controlled use.

To avoid taking "the first one" and running the risk of a serious relapse, it is important to recognize the warning signs of impending trouble and identify the things that make people

relapse. One of these is discouragement. As we've seen, abstinence doesn't magically solve everything. With abstinence, your
most important problems—the ones caused by your dependence—are eliminated, and you are in much better shape to deal
with life's other problems. Really getting your life together,
and minimizing the chance of a slip, requires several things:

- Overcoming your conditioning, breaking the pattern of
  stimulus and response that leads to drug taking;

- Restoring your body, taking care of it, strengthening it,
  using and enjoying it in new ways;

- Finding alternative activities, interests, pleasures, and
  associations;

- Learning to handle anxiety and depression;

- Dealing with the changing relationships that are the result
  of both your drug abuse and your efforts to quit.

This is no overnight program. And while you're working on
it, you may become discouraged that you haven't yet attained
it, that you still are not handling every problem or relationship
smoothly, that you may sometimes or even often feel the urge
to take a drink or a drug. You may find yourself saying, "I'm
not getting better. This isn't working. I need relief. I may as
well give up."

This kind of thinking is a serious warning that you are in
danger of relapsing.

Other warning signs are finding excuses not to go to outpatient group sessions or twelve-step meetings, or "forgetting"
to take your dose of the prescription drug Antabuse. Some
treatment centers use Antabuse to help alcoholics stay off the
bottle during early recovery. As long as you are taking it, the
smallest amount of alcohol will make you violently ill. Usually
you're advised to take it first thing in the morning, before you've
had a chance to spend time thinking about a drink. Some al-

coholism counselors recommend Antabuse for the simple reason that it relieves you of decision making during the most difficult part of recovery. If you take Antabuse every morning, for the rest of that day and at least four days afterward you don't have to decide whether to drink or not; you know you won't because you don't want to suffer the immediate consequences. But of course, you *do* have to decide to take the Antabuse.

It's easy enough to take your pill at first, when you're eager for recovery. But if you find yourself "forgetting" to take your Antabuse for a day or two, then clearly a part of you is thinking about taking a drink. This is a time to reflect on the reasons, and to work on them with the help of your counselor or AA sponsor or group.

Even more serious is deliberately deciding to omit your dose of Antabuse. There may be many motives. You may be having a hard time with personal relationships or at work, and yearning for relief of the pain or tension: "I can't take this anymore. I may just have to have a drink to escape this intolerable tension. I'll stop the Antabuse just for a while until I get over this bad period."

Or maybe the thinking goes something like this: "The annual Christmas party is next week. I'm not going to drink, but I don't want to feel that I *couldn't* even if I wanted to. That would really ruin my enjoyment of the party." Worse still is this: "I'm not going to take Antabuse because I want to drink at the party. But I won't drink anything after the party. In three or four days, when the alcohol is out of my system, I'll go back to Antabuse." The problem is, it just about *never* works that way. After the party, there's always another excuse for postponing Antabuse another day. Or perhaps you'd like to start taking Antabuse again, but you can't get back to a safe starting point— even one drink prevents it. By continuing to drink, you're actively sabotaging your preventive medicine.

Relapse can be triggered by a variety of influences that can be summed up in the phrase "people, places, and things." For the most part, this refers to anyone or any situation associated with drinking or taking drugs; these are known to stir up conditioned desires for drink or drugs.

Being around people who were associated with your drinking or drug behavior can be very dangerous. It is nearly always recommended that you stay away from those friends with whom you used to drink or take drugs, at least until your recovery is more consolidated. You may think to yourself that you can't give up your good friends; but it might be helpful to ask yourself how "good" these friends really were, whether they were "good" friends in the best sense or only good friends in the drinking and drug-taking environment. The test is whether they can accept you and be your friend in other activities than drinking or drug taking. If not, then they aren't such good friends that you can't do without them.

Many people who are determined to remain abstinent have difficulty dealing with social situations where other people are indulging themselves and inviting them to do likewise.

We have all experienced those busybody hosts and hostesses who insist that all guests share in the "goodies." They become mortally insulted if you turn down anything they offer. But remember, they have no mysterious power over you; they cannot make you eat or drink *anything*!

In most cases a simple "No thank you" will do when you're offered cigarettes, joints, lines, pipes, or syringes. With alcohol, you can usually find or ask for an alternative, such as seltzer, tonic water, fruit juice, or soda.

You may be afraid to go to a party or you go and you're afraid not to drink or take drugs because people will sneer at you or be uncomfortable around you. This is more egotistical than realistic. The simple, hard truth is that in most social gatherings, if you are not busy feeling sorry for yourself, you'll discover two things: no one else is feeling sorry for you, and unless you're making your sobriety an important topic of conversation, no one else deeply cares whether or not you're taking intoxicants. In other words, the worst social consequences of abstinence are in the eyes of the unhappy abstainer. The sense of being a social cripple is usually a projection. If not, you're probably just in the wrong place. If you're among people who can only talk to one another once they're loaded, your sobriety *will* make them uncomfortable, and by the same token their intoxication will make *you* uncomfortable. If you're the only one not intent on getting drunk or stoned, and if this creates a problem, it's time for you to leave.

One of the great benefits of the current passion for fitness and health is that more and more people who are not addicts are also staying away from chemical substances. Drinking and taking drugs is no longer so fashionable or so much the norm as it was ten years ago; abstaining doesn't make everybody suspicious that you have "a problem." Health and fitness consciousness has also led many people to shun alcohol except on special occasions, if even then.

Assuming that you have told the truth to your family and closest friends, and assuming that people you encounter casually at a party will not raise their eyebrows at your glass of sparkling water, your only problem is likely to be with questions from people who know you just well enough to know you did drink and to notice that you aren't drinking now, but who don't know you well enough to guess or to be told why. You have a whole range of possible responses when someone says "Not drinking?" or "Seltzer? How come?"

You can brush it off with, "I'm on a diet. Too many calories." Or blame it on your blood-pressure medication. "Just lost my taste for that stuff" will also work, if you don't mind the faint suggestion that the person you're talking to has poor taste because she is drinking that stuff. You don't need to make up an elaborate story or explain in detail; in fact, you definitely shouldn't.

A brief comment from you should end the conversation, and chances are that the same person will promptly forget you ever drank and won't raise the issue again. But there will be times when these replies won't work.

For example, you are absolutely bound to encounter situations where even people who know that you are recovering will refuse to believe that you can't have just one, or who, for perverse though probably unconscious motives, want to test you or even watch you fall on your face. These are the people who say, "Oh, go ahead, just one won't hurt you," or "Just try it." The only answer to this is to say firmly and seriously, "I already tried it."

Except for that happily rare individual who is truly malicious or blindly jealous of your success, or who has some reason for wanting you to be ruined, most people will surprise you by their response to your seriousness and determination. At first they may be disbelieving, but if you stand firm, you will notice the dawning of not only belief but respect. It is also surprising how many people will respond to your attitude by saying, "You know, I really ought to give it up myself." Usually they are not totally serious about this; it is a thought that has probably flitted across their minds on occasion and your behavior has brought it back more forcibly. You may be tempted to grab them and lead them immediately to a rehabilitation center or your twelve-step meeting. Resist the temptation. They are not really ready, or they would be there, and pressure from you ahead of time will make them resent what they see as prose-lytizing, "do-goodism," or forcing their hand. You may say quietly, "If you ever decide, let me know. I'll be glad to help." Then drop it. You should know from your own experience that nobody gives up until *he* has made the decision internally. A premature attempt to help will make him turn against you and make you feel you have failed—another great trigger for relapse.

What is especially threatening is that some people may deliberately attempt to sabotage your recovery. This could be a family member who's resistant to any change in the status quo, or a friend or acquaintance who is envious that you're succeeding at something they haven't even tried. Actively resist this sabotage! With the advice and help of your counselor or sponsor, you should confront such a person with the problem, explain to her the effect their behavior has on you, and show her that you understand she has problems with your dependence too— but make it clear to them that your life is at stake.

Resentment is a particularly destructive emotion because it involves turning your anger inward, rather than expressing it or resolving it by dealing with the source of it. One recovering chemical dependent who sought counseling to avoid what he was sure was an imminent relapse said he was choking with unresolved anger and resentment, at everything and everybody, and really didn't understand why. He was resentful of employees who couldn't do certain tasks as quickly or efficiently as he could do them himself, even though he was aware that he had far more years of practice and experience than they. He would seethe with anger at people who got in grocery express lanes with only one item over the limit, and even found himself "absolutely outraged with resentment against drivers in front of me who held me up because they wouldn't turn right on red." With counseling and discussion with his group, he began to realize that his real anger was against his family. He felt they were not giving him the understanding and support in his recovery that he expected from them. He also felt that while he was changing, they were still doing the same things and treating him the same way they had when he was on drugs. But he had been unable to find ways of discussing this with them and resolving it.

Then there is just the piling up of the little exasperations and frustrations of daily life. The Canadian physician Hans Selye, the developer of the modern stress concept, has pointed out that people can have an overwhelming major stress, such as a death in the family, which he called "local stress." But equally damaging could be a culmination of the building-up of small stresses, which Selye called "general stress," and what most of us would call "the last straw." Either of these kinds of stress can be an invitation to relapse. The growth of insight and of life-management strategies that comes with extended recovery will help you to deal with these in time. During early recovery, the best defense is regular and frequent counseling, constant contact with a twelve-step group, and a close relationship with a sponsor.

The power of these programs in dealing with stress and life problems is summed up in the words of one man who described how prolonged absence from twelve-step meetings reduced his ability to deal with frustration and annoyance: "When I haven't been going to regular meetings, I notice that everybody starts driving weirdly."

The "places and things" that may set off the relapse process include any site or even situation that is associated with your past chemical use. People have widely different opinions about whether the alcoholic or drug user should totally avoid all such places. For the cocaine user, this is not only easier to do (since cocaine, after all, is not generally dispensed at every bar, restaurant, and grocery store, or at every social gathering you may want to attend) but it is more important. Cocaine users are exceptionally sensitive to environmental "cues" that bring on remembered highs and the associated craving. For the alcoholic, the situation is quite different. Alcohol is ubiquitous. The Alcoholics Anonymous "Big Book," the original guide written by the founders of AA, has this to say:

> People have said we must not go where liquor is served; we must not have it in our homes; we must shun friends who drink; we must avoid moving pictures which show drinking scenes; we must not go into bars; our friends must hide their bottles if we go to their houses; we mustn't think or be reminded about alcohol at all. Our experience shows us this is not necessarily so.
>
> We meet these conditions every day. An alcoholic who cannot meet them still has an alcoholic mind . . . his only chance for sobriety would be some place like the Greenland

ice cap, and even there an Eskimo might show up with a bottle of Scotch and ruin everything! . . .

In our belief any scheme of combating alcoholism which proposes to shield the sick man from temptation is doomed to failure. If the alcoholic tries to shield himself he may succeed for a time, but he usually winds up with a bigger explosion than ever . . . These attempts to do the impossible have always failed.

So our rule is not to avoid a place where there is drinking, *if we have a legitimate reason for being there.*

In early recovery, however, it is safer to stay away from temptation entirely. This is not the time to experiment. Eventually, when your recovery is more consolidated, there will be people and places you can't or don't wish to avoid until you have the strength and the skills to encounter them without discomfort or danger. As recovery proceeds, you can gradually work your way back into these situations. Begin with an inventory of all such places, classifying them from least tempting to most dangerous. Then slowly and cautiously you try out the easiest situation, working your way carefully up the scale. The minute you begin to feel uncomfortable, get out and slow down, or stop at that level and don't go on at all. In fact, there will be places at the top of the list where you will never need or want to go and where you shouldn't ever go. For example, you will need to attend family wedding receptions, but you don't have to stop off at the bar after work. You may need to attend the company's annual awards dinner, but you don't need to eat in the restaurant where you always spent the predinner hour having cocktails. And actively seeking out old drug-using friends or places where people handle paraphernalia and drugs is definitely hazardous and unnecessary. The "legitimate reason" rule of AA applies very strongly here.

This raises what can be a troubling issue for many recovering alcoholics, if not for other chemically dependent people: what to do about a job that involves much socializing focused on drink (or more rarely, pot or cocaine).

A change of job might become necessary if it is clear that to return to the same job might increase the risk of relapse. Even a job with a high level of stress, boredom, or frustration may be too much for a recently recovered chemical dependent to handle. Equally a problem is a job that entails frequent socializing at bars or parties, or regular "expense account" lunches, banquets, and conventions where alcohol is an outstanding feature of the entertainment. In some cases the drinking is not an integral part of the job, but custom involves stopping at the bar after work with customers or fellow workers to have "one for the road." Whether to continue in such a job is a highly individual matter. Much depends on how "antsy" you get in these situations, whether you are involved in effective aftercare or whether you have a strong support system such as a twelve-step group. The decision may also rest with how difficult it would be for you to find a comparable job that didn't involve drinking; in some cases, it might even be preferable to take a lower salary or a somewhat less satisfying job at least until recovery and sobriety are well established. After all, recovery is vastly more important than that particular job; if you relapse, you may end up with no job at all. If you do remain on such a job, you should deliberately and consciously apply all the relapse-preventive techniques available.

Sometimes the people, places, or things may entail one particular responsibility or pleasure that you think you cannot forgo or that is the hardest of all to forgo. A couple of examples of this: the alcoholic who appreciates fine wines and enjoys them for the taste, not just for the alcohol in them, whose best friends are the members of a wine-tasting club, and who feels she can give up all forms of alcohol except her once-a-month club meeting; and the teenager whose only friends are those who smoke pot or occasionally use cocaine, and who sees no possibility of getting any other friends in his school or neighborhood. To choose to stay in these situations practically guarantees relapse; there is really no choice but to relinquish the club and to find new friends. It will be a painful choice, but the alternative will be even worse. This is the place to apply two slogans that are popular among recovering people:

"Winners do what they *have* to do;
losers do what they *want* to do."
and
"If you don't want to slip, stay away from slippery places."

Among many techniques and strategies for preventing relapse, one of the first is to know yourself and your moods. Certain moods can act as a reminder of your experiences with drink or drugs, either alone or in combination with other conditioned stimuli. Some gradually lose the response to relapse-triggering cues or stimuli except when they are in a particular mood—usually anger, depression, or anxiety. It's essential to recognize which moods make you most susceptible to cravings or thinking about drink or drugs.

Except for that, your moods in recovery will generally be very different from those you experienced while you were still drinking or taking drugs, so you will have to start over again learning how you generally feel, what brings on certain moods, how you react to disappointment or insults or other mood changers. Once you have recognized your "normal" patterns of feeling, you will be better able to detect signs of what has been called BUD—or building up to drink (or drugs).

"Creeping" Relapse

Relapse is not usually something that just comes and hits you in the face; it is more often a gradual process that can creep up on you before you know it, unless you are aware and alert. The "buildup" may begin with unexpected or unexplained irritability, boredom, restlessness, or just feeling at odds with yourself. If these feelings don't go away or you can't make them go away, you may begin to feel out of control. This may bring you to a second stage, of withdrawing from the activities you have initiated to replace your old drinking and drug-taking habits. You may begin to go back to your feelings of denial, that your habit wasn't such a bad one, that you aren't really like "those other people who really do have a problem." You may find it harder to remember the bad effects of your habit and begin thinking about the good ones. You may feel confused, alienated from the new pattern of living you have been trying to forge. You are now well on your way into the "buildup" and on to relapse.

This time of irritability and restlessness is the moment to get back into the safety of your support group, to talk it over with them or with someone else who will be understanding and helpful, such as an AA sponsor, a clergyman, or a best friend. Talking it over and reaching out for help, in fact, are major lines of defense in relapse prevention.

Finally, it is essential to deal with one of the greatest of all threats to abstinence and obstacles to recovery: guilt, and the feelings of shame and worthlessness from succumbing to drink or drugs. Most chemically dependent people fail to see that their drug use or drinking was not a failure of character but a genetically encouraged, misguided effort to cope with the problems of life. They focus exclusively on the horrible things they did while under the influence, use this obsession as a means of punishing themselves. Society's low opinion of them feeds their own poor self-images so that they see themselves as weak, defective, and despicable human beings.

To counteract this demands new ways of looking at yourself and seeking good advice and guidance on how to foster a healthier self-image and self-esteem. One of the best ways of doing this is to substitute workable coping methods for the older, inefficient ones. Often this requires a careful assessment of the situation so that you can get a clear idea of what the problem is that you are trying to solve.

An example is the man who drank a lot after work, particularly when he was on a job out of town. His experience persuaded him that this allowed him to unload a lot of job stress. Because it relaxed him, he felt that he was able to think more clearly at the end of the day's stress and could thus "recharge" and be better prepared for the next day. He also thought it improved his memory. This conviction was a strong deterrent to his recovery. However, he was persuaded to try some alternatives to drinking, such as physical exercise and deep muscle relaxation. He learned very quickly that he could relax effectively this way, have an even clearer head, and better memory than when he was drinking.

The "active ingredient" in his clear thinking and memory was not alcohol; it was relaxation. This discovery freed him from his expectation that without alcohol he would not do as well on the job—just through developing alternative skills for managing stress.

Gaining Coping Skills

Coping with the relapse problem requires specific skills and techniques.

One reason many people find it painful and difficult to maintain sobriety—especially in the beginning—is that they just don't know how. Relying on willpower certainly won't do it. What you need are the growth and discovery you gain from twelve-step meetings and aftercare, supported by the tools or techniques to translate these lessons into action.

There is a television show on which a man demonstrates how to paint a picture, step by step, and in careful detail—whether you should start with sky or land, when you should pick up the paint on the end of the bristles and when you dip the whole brush in, where to use long sweeping strokes and when to dab. It's almost astonishing to watch him create, in half an hour, a finished oil painting, complete with sky, clouds, hills, trees, flowers, a stream with ducks in it, and a waterfall.

You or I might make up our minds that we, too, could paint, and could be *determined* to do it. But we couldn't if we didn't learn his techniques. His paintings aren't great—he is not an artistic or creative genius—but even if you or I had more innate artistic talent we couldn't paint better. We couldn't even paint as well. Because we don't know *how*; we don't know the technique, the tricks of the trade.

No more could a person who has never skied before make it safely down an expert slope just by gritting his teeth and saying, "I will do it!"

Of course it looks easy. Anything looks easy when it's being done by someone who knows how. Just stop and think a moment the next time you tie your shoes. It's something you could do in your sleep, it's so easy. But remember how hard it was when you tried it the first time as a child?

If tying a shoelace or painting a landscape or skiing downhill are difficult if not impossible until you know the strategies, why would people think they can handle the incredibly tough job of abstinence without any techniques or tools?

That's why you can't just go to your favorite niece's wedding totally unprepared and untrained for that moment when the glasses are being raised for toasts and your sister-in-law fixes you with a glare and says, "Why aren't you toasting the bride and groom?" You have to know *how* not to drink; you have to know what to say to your sister-in-law. You need to know *before* you get to the wedding. *Before* you run into your ex–best friend with whom you use to share the joints and pass around the mirror and he says it's been so long since you've gotten together and why don't you come on over, he's expecting a few of the old crowd. *Before* you're cleaning out the cupboards on a day when you're really stressed and tense and you just by amazing coincidence discover a long-forgotten stash of Valium or that hidden "emergency" pint of vodka.

And for really serious challenges to your good intentions, you need practice. Nobody ties a shoelace very neatly on the first try.

There have been many studies of what makes some people succeed in achieving and maintaining abstinence: they make it absolutely clear that the secret is "coping," and the secret to coping is coping *strategies*. None of these studies reveals absolutely which strategies work best; it seems to vary a lot from one person to the next. But the evidence is clear that "just using willpower" is the least successful coping strategy. Even more undeniably and dramatically clear is just using one strategy or just using a couple of strategies now and then doesn't work. The more coping techniques you know, the more strategies you use, and the more often you use them, the easier it will become, and the more successful you will be. What is the most heartening thing about all of this is that these are not just strategies that keep you from relapsing. Most of them are techniques for improving your way of life, for growing, for becoming a better human being.

The relapse-preventing and recovery-fostering techniques you will need are those that not only help you to resist temptation but also cope with stress—since stress is often such an important factor in relapse. There are two basic kinds of coping skills: cognitive or thinking and behavioral or acting. A person who feels on the verge of a relapse begins to examine the reasons why temptation is so strong at the moment: boredom, for instance. That's the cognitive half. The behavioral half is going to the local hospital asking for work as a volunteer, or taking up some interesting hobby or exciting sport. Let's start with a set of six cognitive skills—delay, minimization, distraction, reinforcement, thinking of consequences, and problem solving.

Delay: Just "waiting out" the craving, the panic, or the feeling that you can't stand another minute without a drink or a drug. Dr. Peter Miller, who runs the Sea Pines Behavioral Institute in South Carolina recommends this rule for self-restraint: "Immediately impose a ten-minute delay on any decision regarding the temptation." This allows time for cravings to subside, and lets you consider the consequences of your actions so you can make a more logical decision. You could also use those ten minutes to call a support person.

Minimization or *selective comparison:* Think it over and assure yourself that the abstinence is not really *that* uncomfortable, particularly compared to the consequences of relapse. Remember how bad a hangover felt, or missing work because of a drug binge. Reminding yourself that the temptation you're feeling now isn't nearly so bad as the aftereffects of a binge.

Distraction: Turn your attention elsewhere; think about positive activities—meditating, praying, reading.

Reinforcement: Remind yourself how successful you've been so far in your efforts at recovery. List in your mind all the benefits you've gotten from abstinence.

Thinking of consequences: Go over all the negative things that would happen if you went back to drink or drugs.

Problem solving or *decision making:* Figure out why you are suffering stress, look at various alternative actions, and decide what course to take.

These strategies are a good example of cognitive therapy, because they involve constructive changes in how we mentally approach and react to a situation. Conversely, behavioral strategies concern our actions, not thoughts. Hence behavioral strategies involve attendance at meetings, withdrawal from a situation, self-assertion, support seeking, self-monitoring, alternative behavior, relaxation techniques, healthful eating and drinking, physical fitness, and acceptance. The cognitive and behavioral strategies complement each other; in many cases, the behavioral strategies involve taking whatever action you decided on prior to entering a difficult situation.

Attend meetings: Alcoholics Anonymous, Cocaine Anonymous, or Narcotics Anonymous. Experts and recovered chemical dependents almost universally agree that these twelve-step groups are without question the single most effective road to recovery.

Withdraw: Get out of the situation entirely. For example, if your stress is coming from a job and you cannot change the nature of the job or negotiate the problem with your supervisor or co-workers, the solution may be to transfer to another department or to find another job. Staying away from drinking or drug-taking associates and locations is another very effective withdrawal strategy for preventing relapse. Many people feel it is absolutely necessary to remove all liquor, prescription drugs or other drugs from the home, and in studies of relapse prevention, this technique was used by a larger number of those who remained abstinent than among those who relapsed. It may be necessary to compromise a little and allow a spouse or other family member to have alcohol in the home for specific occasions, but any leftovers should be removed promptly.

Be assertive: Stand up for yourself. For many people this may simply be a matter of setting boundaries or limits; for example, agreeing to work a certain amount of overtime but making it clear that your job description and pay do not justify your supervisor keeping you late every single day; telling your wife to stay within her household budget or telling your husband that you can't hold down a job, keep house, raise the children, *and* combat your dependence all at the same time unless he lends a hand with some of the chores—such as driving the kids to the dentist or picking up the clothes from the dry cleaner (but not necessarily that cliché "husband's job"—emptying the garbage, and so on); telling your best friend he can borrow your car once more but only if he brings it back when promised—with the gas tank refilled. Sometimes assertiveness can be something as simple as not allowing your dinnertime to be interrupted by nonemergency phone calls. It's important to learn how to tell friends and relatives (politely) that you can't talk right now and will call back in fifteen minutes or half an hour. Asserting yourself in these small ways not only gives you practice for the big things, but cuts down on all these little daily frustrations that can add up to a big stress total. For the chemically dependent, assertiveness in particular means saying a firm "No thank you" to all enticements from your drinking or drug-taking friends.

Become social and get expert support: Seek help from other people, either emotional support through talking over your problems with a sympathetic friend, or practical support through direct advice and guidance from a counselor or support group. Studies have shown that people who remained continuously sober without relapse after rehabilitation were those who were most actively involved in twelve-step programs immediately after treatment and were intensely involved in aftercare programs or treatment; in fact aftercare appeared to be critical in resisting relapse. The most significant differences between people who remained abstinent and those who relapsed had to do with whether the person used his/her sponsor and whether he/she "reached out" to other twelve-step members when tense and in need of help. "Sharing of self and helping each other" was very important.

Give yourself support: Self-support covers several very effective methods. One is self-monitoring, or keeping track of your moods, your episodes of craving, your return to any behavior that was closely associated with your drinking or drug use. Monitoring gives you a better understanding of yourself and better control over your day-to-day feelings and behavior. Self-reinforcement is also useful; giving a mental compliment or a real reward for progress or for success in applying other techniques.

Practice alternative behavior: One of the absolutely best solutions to stress or temptation is work. A satisfying job is ideal; a less than satisfying job is still better than no job at all, just as part-time work is not as good as full-time but better than nothing. If for some reason you can't work for pay, any other kind of work will do; for instance, volunteer jobs or work around the house or grounds. Jobs that entail service to other people are especially valuable.

Exercise is a great stress reducer and relapse preventer. It takes time, it makes you feel and look good, and it enhances your self-esteem. Hobbies that require activity (as opposed, for instance, to just collecting matchbook covers wherever you go) are also useful. Weekends and evenings often present a heightened danger of relapse, since many drinkers and drug users never developed adequate skills for spending leisure time in a rewarding fashion. These times should be planned ahead with enjoyable or satisfying activities that are different from what you had been doing with your leisure; for instance, going to a sporting event or going bowling rather than sitting at home watching TV. Twelve-step meetings are an excellent alternative to empty time.

Relax: Through muscle-relaxing exercises, biofeedback, lying back and listening to music, taking a warm bath or shower, asking a family member to massage your back, or through prayer or meditation, practice relaxation.

It appears that all psychoactive drugs affect us by mimicking the action of naturally occurring enzymes produced by our own bodies. If this is true, why can't we learn to use our own minds and bodies to gain the positive effects that we tried to get through the use of alcohol and other drugs? Many recovering people have learned to do just that through meditation and prayer.

Develop flexibility: Getting rid of rigidity. People with a chemical dependence often start out with inflexible personalities or develop them as a result of the dependence. When you're on drink or drugs, you begin to develop certain habits of mind and behavior that begin to seem like the only way to do things; you cannot accept the possibility of alternatives. But rigidity, though it may seem strong, is in fact very fragile. As anyone knows who has watched trees in a hurricane, the stiff hardwoods are the ones to break first, not the swaying palms that give with the force of the wind.

Rigidity in abstinence often snaps against the force of drink or drug hunger and the urgings of well-meaning friends to have one for old times' sake. "Drugs may cause stress, but the rigidity of white-knuckle sobriety can cause just as much stress." Relapses rarely occur on the premise of "now I'm going to go out and get loaded." More often it is a matter of not being flexible enough to accept alternative thoughts and actions, of insisting on doing things the same old way—which didn't work in the first place. Sometimes even thinking so hard that it would be insane to take a drink or drug can freeze the mind or make it "stick," leaving no room for maneuvering, for problem solving or for coping techniques; so in fact you do just what it is you're concentrating so hard on *not* doing.

Eat and drink healthily: Have a favorite snack or nonalcoholic liquid instead of whatever it is you're craving. Some alcoholics feel at a loss without a drink in their hands, especially at the end of the day or their usual drinking time. Keep a drink in your hand: seltzer or mineral water or fruit juice. Refill it when it's empty. You won't miss the glass of alcohol so much, and you need plenty of liquids to be healthy and help restore nutritional balance.

Be health-minded: Concentration on restoring fitness. Feeling well is an excellent defense against relapse. Early recovery is an excellent time to take stock, to learn and practice good nutrition, to join a health club or start your own fitness program. Simple exercise equipment—light weights, jumping rope, an exercise bicycle—can duplicate many of the routines used in expensive clubs. Videotaped workouts are inexpensive and useful. Looking after your appearance is an adjunct to this; looking well along with feeling well can be a great boost to morale.

Seek acceptance: Addiction is a problem that can't be immediately solved or a situation that can't be immediately changed. Many people find in religion, or through prayers for help and guidance, a way to get past insuperable difficulties. The "serenity prayer" used by AA is considered by many people one of the strongest and most often used aids to coping and continued recovery: "God grant me the serenity to accept what I cannot change, the courage to change what I can, and the wisdom to know the difference."

6

ADDICTIVE ATTACHMENTS

ALCOHOLISM AND DRUG ABUSE HAVE BEEN CALLED "EQUAL opportunity destroyers." They destroy everybody they touch, without discriminating. But what they touch most powerfully is the family.

That's why addiction is always a family affair. Your dependence influences and is influenced by your family, and it will influence your children and their families. Even if you have no family of your own right now, you came from a family. That family influenced the development of *your* dependence.

This is particularly true of alcoholism, which threatens children in the family with its genetically influenced, physical susceptibility to alcohol along with the emotional and psychological damage associated with having an alcoholic parent.

Virtually every alcoholic comes from a family in which there has been alcoholism. Many families will deny this, and in fact, there may not be any alcoholics in the immediate family. But if you talk to enough people and listen long enough, eventually you will unearth the admission that "Well, father did like his beer, but of course, so did all his friends." Or "We never thought of Aunt Emily as having a problem. I mean, she did often have to take naps in the afternoon, and sometimes she was a little muddle headed." But the families of drug users and those addicted to prescription medicines also suffer emotional crippling. All of them need help.

The Codependent Prison

The disease suffered by families of the chemically dependent is called "codependency," because family members become as dependent on the sick family system as the real dependent becomes on his or her chemical of choice. They are as imprisoned in it as the dependent is imprisoned by chemicals. And they feed each other's dependencies.

In particular, the families of the chemically dependent become so enmeshed with the dependent that they help perpetuate the dependence and often either unwittingly interfere or deliberately sabotage the dependent's attempts to recover.

That is why your recovery requires that the family also recover. It may seem unfair, but the reverse is not true. Family members can recover without the recovery of the chemically dependent person; in fact, if you are not in treatment or trying to recover, they must go ahead with their own recovery regardless. Many codependents go into treatment or counseling thinking that the purpose is to get their addicted family member clean. They find it difficult to admit they also have a problem. They also find it difficult to accept that the dependent's problem is the dependent's problem and has to be dealt with by him or her, but the codependent's problem doesn't hinge on whether the dependent is recovering or not. They can and should give support or help if the dependent is trying to recover, but they can't force the recovery or control it or make it a necessary part of their own recovery. If the chemically dependent person isn't trying to recover, other family members must go ahead on their own. The ideal, of course, is for everyone in the family to work on recovery at the same time; not together in the same treatment program, but concurrently. Because you are all trapped in the addiction together, you need to understand and recognize your family's needs for recovery, and they need to understand their own pain and work on their own recovery as well as understand and help you with yours. As a recovering alcoholic or drug user, you will have a tremendous disadvantage in recovery if you must continue to deal with codependents who are stuck in the old ways of feeling and behaving.

If you are the child of a parent who is alcoholic or drug-dependent, you will need to deal with the problems this family relationship has caused you. In the case of alcoholics, in particular, recovery may depend a lot on solving the problems common to adult children of alcoholics (see pages 157–66). It has been said that "within a great many alcoholics lies an untreated codependent. If the chemical dependence is treated but not the codependence that contributed to it in the first place, all you get is another dry drunk."

If you have children, you will need to respect their needs and understand the problems your illness has caused them. If you are married but childless, your spouse will be the significant person in your recovery and will need help with his or her own recovery. This is not going to be easy for anybody. You have all suffered, you are all confused, angry, resentful, and undoubtedly locked into the family's system of denial.

Understanding your disease is as difficult for your family, in spite of their familiarity with it, as it is for anybody who doesn't have it. People simply do not easily recognize or accept that what appears to be totally *abnormal* behavior—getting drunk or stoned or high—is due to your disease, which makes you continue to use chemicals in order to feel *normal*; that is, relieved from tension, craving, withdrawal symptoms, and so on. And if you're really working hard at recovery and fighting to fend off relapse, you may find it difficult to understand why they don't give you more credit and more sympathy. They may also find it difficult to accept your recovery and your determination as real; they've heard too many promises before.

The "Rules" of Codependency

In a family where there is an addict, all family members are seriously handicapped because they are stuck in the patterns and abnormal "rules" that dependent families create and rely on.

The most fundamental rule is "Don't feel." This is our old enemy denial again, only in a new situation. It is central to the definition of codependence: "an emotional, psychological, and behavioral condition that develops as a result of an individual's prolonged exposure to and practice of a set of oppressive rules— rules that prevent the open expression of feeling as well as the direct discussion of personal and interpersonal problems." These rules are numerous, sometimes complicated, and always self-defeating. They're adopted as "home remedies" to cope with a situation that nobody can cope with in a healthy way. When the remedies don't work and things get worse, family members continue with these home remedies, only more frantically. This just creates more problems, which everybody tries to solve in the same old way, and the pattern repeats itself, becoming more and more habitual and self-destructive.

The second rule is "Don't talk." Because the system is based on denial, it imposes silence and distance on each person involved. Because it makes the family so concentrated in on itself, it throws up a wall between itself and the rest of the world. What results is a family that is closed not only to each other but to everyone else. The contrast to a healthy, loving, "open" family is striking.

In the open family, there is room to grow and expand and a desire for others to grow. Family members have separate interests, other friends, other warm and enduring relationships. They encourage each other to grow and reach out, because they are secure in their own worth and aren't threatened by the other's self-sufficiency. They trust each other and respect each other's integrity. They are willing to be themselves and to take risks, to explore feelings in and out of the family relationship. They are also able to enjoy being alone. Yes, there really are families like this; yours can be one of them.

In the closed family of the alcoholic or drug user, by contrast, people depend heavily on each other for security and the re-assurance of shared denial, and they use this intensity of need as proof of love (instead of recognizing it as a sign of fear, insecurity, and loneliness). They are totally involved with each other, neglect old friends and outside interests, and have a strictly limited social life. They are preoccupied with each oth-er's behavior and lean entirely on each other's approval for a sense of their own identity and self-worth. They're jealous, possessive, and cannot tolerate separations except after a fight. They gain reassurance from repeated, ritualized behavior, and frequently suspend their own needs and deprive themselves for the sake of the other—or else are so preoccupied with their own needs they don't even recognize that others have needs. They try to eliminate all possible risks and to build perfect protection against hurt.

Most of all, codependent families deny that any of this is true; they deny that the dependent has a problem or that the co-dependents have one; they deny that they are feeling pain. They often don't even know they are *feeling* pain. They deny the need for change and are more afraid of it even than most nondepen-dent people. Therefore . . .

The third rule is "Don't change." In fact, people do not usually make important life changes unless they become aware that they will lose some invaluable thing if they do not change. Some people call this "hitting the wall" or "kissing concrete," phrases adopted from runners' descriptions of a marathon, usually around the twentieth mile, when going on is like smashing into a concrete wall. But as far as dependents are concerned, I call it facing reality.

The thing alcoholics or addicts might not want to lose but are in danger of losing is *everything*—from a job to loved ones to life itself. The thing codependents are most likely to lose but shouldn't want to is their sense of self; a life of their own, freedom of spirit, and self-respect.

In order to save themselves, the dependent and the codependent must first recognize and admit the hard reality of their lives. When you are caught up in chemical dependence, you are so busy covering things up you probably can't see what is happening. It helps to look at what goes on in codependent families so that you can uncover what is going on in yours.

The Dynamics of Codependent Families

While every member of a family is affected, they're affected in different ways. The adult codependent may feel trapped, but in fact does have the alternative of escape; the child actually is trapped and can't easily run away. Adults learn to adapt and cope with difficulties; they already have some experience of life and some skills in dealing with relationships. Children, particularly young ones, haven't learned yet but are in the process of learning, and what they learn in the codependent family is all the wrong lessons. Children aren't born with moral values, social skills, or standards for evaluating behavior. They learn from example—and in the codependent family, the example they see is dishonesty, distrust, manipulation, unresolved anger, suppressed resentment, coldness, silence, and a host of poor problem-solving techniques.

The adult spouse, on the other hand, tries to apply what has been learned through experience in order to adapt to this unhealthy situation. Yet little of what life has taught will have provided the tools and the wisdom to cope with it in a healthy, effective way. Instead, the adult spouse generally turns to the

simplest (and most socially acceptable) means at hand: denying
the problem while at the same time trying to control it. The
first makes it impossible to admit the need for help, the second
is impossible in itself and makes it impossible for the spouse to
recognize and try to meet his or her own needs. As the dependent spouse's problem progresses, these tools become more and
more destructive.

The most significant of all differences between adults and
children in the codependent family, however, is this: the psychological damage to an adult is imposed on someone who has
already developed a personality, a character, an individuality.
No matter how many changes an adult undergoes during codependence, the basic nature is still there and can be restored
with effort and help. The child, on the other hand, suffers the
psychological and emotional blows while his or her character
is developing. Sadly, the abnormal responses and learning patterns may become so embedded that they are much harder to
dislodge than in a codependent adult. That is a compelling reason for getting *early* help for the children of alcoholics and drug
users, and for dependents to seek recovery early.

Codependence develops in direct parallel with chemical dependence. As the dependent (for the sake of example, let's say
it's the husband) becomes more focused and concentrated on
getting and using alcohol or drugs, the codependent (his wife)
becomes more focused on him and begins to change her behavior in response. She begins trying to control his chemical
use, monitoring it frequently, and meanwhile struggling to keep
peace in the marriage and to shield him from the shock and
disapproval of family members, friends, and his employer. Like
him, she learns to lie to everybody, including herself, as the
focus shifts more and more toward him. As he increasingly
loses control over chemical use, she loses control over her own
behavior, moods, emotions, and reactions. Then she works
even harder to strengthen her defenses by repressing her feelings, taking responsibility for everything, acting cheerful, an-
esthetizing pain by pretending it doesn't exist, and numbing

her emotional reactions. To maintain some sense of self-esteem, she begins to feel righteous, even proud, about her strength and ability to "put up with all of this." By taking on the work of denial and protection, she *relinquishes to him* all control and power over her feelings and behavior—thus helping to *perpetuate his dependence*.

Alternatively, she may exact penance from him by taking on so much responsibility that he becomes emotionally subservient. This weakens his self-esteem still further, and thrusts him deeper into his dependence. Throughout all this, the wife grows resentful and frustrated, becoming less and less patient and tolerant of her husband's behavior. Nevertheless, having accepted the responsibility for "helping" him, she becomes more involved and less able to take care of, or even recognize, her own needs.

Here are some of the things a codependent spouse may feel or do:

- Take a job or a second job to get away from the problem and/or maintain financial security

- Become less open and honest because of resentment, anger, and hurt feelings

- Avoid sexual contact

- Overprotect the children, neglect them, and/or use them for emotional support

- Gradually become socially withdrawn and isolated

- Lose feelings of self-respect and self-worth

- Take alcohol or prescription drugs in the hope of relief.

A classic description of the clues to a diagnosis of codependence in the children or spouses of addicts was stated by Don Wegscheider, in *If Only My Parents Understood Me*:

- Super-responsibility: "If I don't take care of things, they just won't get done."

- Pseudofragility: "I don't know how much more of this I can take!"

- Hypochondria: "I hardly get over one cold when I catch another."

- Powerlessness: "I've tried everything to get him to stop."

- Self-blame: "I should have planned for that."

These are all defensive postures by which a codependent avoids looking honestly at his/her position and doing something about it.

The codependent may also begin to be a father or mother to the dependent partner, which is a strategy bound to fail. A marriage partner cannot be a parent, and the result will be that both partners will begin to punish each other for not doing a good job as either spouse or as parent.

Most dangerous of all, codependents eventually take on a new identity that swallows up and obliterates their original identity. Codependents become codependents first and foremost, essentially resigning from all other roles in life. Their chief concern and interest is now the dependent, the protection of the denial system, and the effort to survive *within the dependence situation*. They become attached to their new identity and this all-consuming role. Without realizing it, they not only stop trying to fight the dependent's habit, they actually—if unknowingly—do things to maintain it. They make it easier for the dependent to get by with it. They may claim they can't do otherwise. They will even go out and buy alcohol or drugs, saying, "What choice have I got? He's going to do it anyway, whether I buy it or he does," or "If I buy it, I get less than he would if he went out for it." They forgive everything, they reassure the dependent that he isn't an alcoholic or an addict, he just "has a problem" and "he'll get over it once this job hassle (or whatever excuse he uses) is straightened out."

This is called *"enabling."* Its most profound expression is in the spouse's conspiring with the dependent to deny or conceal the illness, sometimes persisting even after the dependent tries to accept the truth. One female patient of mine, seeking help after ten years of alcoholism, said at one point in her dependence that she had faced up to the illness after much inner struggle. She got up the courage to speak to her husband one night at bedtime, saying that she wanted to go to an AA meeting because she felt she was an alcoholic. His reply was brief but firm: "Nonsense. Go to sleep."

The Recovering Codependent

Recovery for the codependent, like recovery for the dependent, is not a do-it-yourself project. It requires professional guidance and the encouragement of other people who are having or have had the same experience. There is nothing remotely equal to the insight and support you can get from those who know exactly what you have gone through. Someone once said that the five most important words in recovery are "I know how you feel." Having others listen to you—probably the first time this has happened to you in years, validates your feelings and erases your sense of being crazy or unique or at fault for everything. Listening to others talk about your feelings takes away your sense of being totally alone and isolated. Seeing other people tending to their own needs and doing something about their own problems helps you to understand that looking after yourself is not selfish—it's necessary, and in the long run it will also be better for the dependent in your life and others in your family. Being around people who freely express their misgivings, their pain, and their successes gives you hope while making it easier for you to stop denying that your life has been hell.

Recovery for a codependent, like recovery for a dependent, begins with the breaking down of denial and the recognition of one's own needs. As long as the codependent is expected to play a role in the recovery of the dependent, without the reverse being expected as well, the "sicker than thou" attitude on the part of the dependent may be perpetuated. This, in turn, perpetuates the "other-centeredness" or lack of identity that is so much a part of the disease of codependence.

The codependent must realize that the issue should no longer be the dependent's "cure" but the codependent's survival.

The work of recovery for codependents has much in common with the work of recovering from dependence—but in general it's easier and happens more rapidly (partly because the codependent doesn't have to fight the battle of abstinence, withdrawal, and cravings).

First, the codependent has to accept the label. This can be a great relief, because the label is like a diagnosis that explains all the crazy symptoms you've been having while at the same time carrying with it the possibility of recovery. When codependents are given a name for what they are experiencing, they can distinguish it from being crazy or stupid or inadequate.

Most codependents aren't aware that they suffer from an illness that's caused by the illness of their partner or parent. They think that they're just normal human beings like anybody else, and they simply don't have the right stuff to deal efficiently with this family problem. They feel like failures because they couldn't get their partner or parent to quit. The truth is, *nobody* can get somebody else to quit unless that person wants to, and the disease of codependence is not a symptom of weakness or poor character. Accepting the label can open a new perspective on life, provide a new framework for understanding the past, and offer hope for a different future.

Second, the codependent must admit the pain. It may be strange that someone who is suffering would persist in denying it, but people in dependent families do all sorts of unthinkable things in their inefficient efforts to achieve some normality—

however false. Denying the pain is part of denying the problem. It is part of the general subduing of feelings and the role-playing and pretending that the codependent uses to ward off reality. It is a milestone in recovery when a codependent can admit and exhibit feelings and discover the powerful truth that it's okay to have feelings; you don't have to hide or stifle them. Such a moment is common in the environment of a twelve-step meeting, when someone comes into the room, another group member asks, "How are you," and the answer is an honest "Lousy," instead of "I'm fine, thanks." Or when the answer is, "I'm so depressed I feel like I might cry any minute," and the other member says, "Go ahead. Here, have some Kleenex."

A few years ago, a recovering codependent shared these feelings with me:

> For so many years I hated to touch anyone, to have to hug them or be hugged. You know, when I'd see a friend or a close relative approaching I'd actually try to stand so they couldn't hug or kiss me—I felt so ugly, so awful about myself that I wanted to spare them the discomfort of being "degraded" by me . . . Recovery means a lot of things to a lot of people, but to me it means finally knowing the feeling of a good hug.

Many codependents become so confused they stop feeling anything at all, or if they can feel, they can't distinguish between different kinds of feelings—is this anger or hurt or fear? Once you can have a feeling and identify it correctly—say, "This is fear!"—then you can figure out what to *do* with that emotion. Your response and your behavior may be very different when you realize that what you thought was "anger" is really "hurt."

Third, the codependent must give up relying on willpower. Using willpower to survive intolerable situations gives the illusion of control over the situation—but it is only an illusion; in truth, everything is completely out of control.

Willpower is useful for some things and totally useless for

others. You may be working at some difficult task and reach a point where you say, "I just can't work another minute." But if it is essential that you finish the job, exerting your willpower can keep you at it until it's completed. You can also "will yourself" to keep silent and hold your tongue on those occasions when releasing your anger would be wrong and hurtful. You can use willpower to bring yourself to make necessary apologies or perform various other unpleasant though essential duties. But an addict *cannot* use willpower alone to stop drinking or taking drugs, and you *cannot* use it to influence another person's emotions or behavior.

In fact, one of the most important basic principles for confronting the problem of codependence is that you cannot change other people's feelings or actions *in any way at all*. Sometimes changes in others happen in response to changes in you, but it never happens in response to any direct attempt by you. Sometimes it may appear that you have caused the change; for example, when a spouse says, "Make up your mind; either me or the drink and drugs," and the dependent says, "Okay, I'll get help." All this means is either that the dependent is bargaining with you, and will soon be right back on the drink or drugs, or that the dependent was ready to recover and your ultimatum was just the excuse that was needed. If the dependent isn't ready, the response to the ultimatum will be, "Fine, go ahead and leave." The change *must* come from within.

This is why codependents, like dependents, can be "dry drunks." They may stop enabling or stop being a martyr by exercising willpower. They can succeed only by gritting their teeth and forcing themselves to it, as long as no fundamental change has occurred—when they not only accept the fact that they are codependents but also accept the truth that they can't control this problem through willpower. They will remain "dry drunks" until they do what has to be done to begin real recovery: give up denial, learn to accept what can't be changed and start learning what can be changed and doing something to change it.

Fourth, codependents must relinquish their "sick" identities and stop playing their "sick" roles—martyr, missionary, victim, and so on. If they don't, codependents will give up struggling entirely and just accept this painful position as all their lot. Then, because the truth is painful, they may try to resign themselves to this by renaming their role in the addicted family "play." Nobody who is used and taken advantage of by other people wants to be considered a "wimp." However, it's quite all right to be an unselfish, devoted, patient, and loyal wife or husband (even if that's just a martyr in disguise).

Having perfected this role, it's frightening to be asked to give it up, especially if you haven't yet figured out what's going to take its place. It feels like no-man's-land. Codependents often resist this as strongly as if they were giving up something truly valuable, and in fact, making the switch does mean work. It means taking responsibility for your behavior and for the restoration of your real self. The great thing about accepting responsibility is that it confers true freedom and gives you some real control over your life. It means acting *for yourself* and your own best interests, not living for what you have mistakenly believed were the best interests of your sick partner.

This sounds selfish. But alcoholism and drug abuse are selfish diseases. And the only antidote for the subjugation of self that characterizes codependent behavior is to refocus on the self in healthy ways.

Many codependents, at some point, think of escape or actually attempt to escape. Some hoard money for that runaway day or even separate temporarily in hopes "something" will happen during the separation. The powerful denial experienced by codependents often takes the form of thinking that breaking off the relationship will make everything okay again. Such codependents are denying their own need for treatment and fail to see that they carry the addictive thinking, responses, and behaviors into other areas of life.

Some codependents walk out and then return; it's like a relapse. It's quite likely to happen if the codependent does nothing else toward recovery except get out; the habits, the compulsion, are too strong.

Some marriages break up for good, and for many complicated reasons. Statistically, it's more likely to be the husband who makes a permanent break from a chemically dependent wife than the other way around.

"In our society today, if a woman is married to a male alcoholic and there are children under the age of eighteen in the family, nine out of ten women will stay with the alcoholic. However, if the situation is reversed, and she is the alcoholic, only one out of ten males will stay."

Why? Sometimes a woman doesn't have any alternatives; if she hasn't been working or hasn't been trained for any kind of a job, it's financially impossible to leave. She might be able to do it alone but not if there are children. Women also feel a much greater obligation in our society, even today, to honor the "in sickness and in health" part of the marriage vow. There is also the fear of being alone and unmarried, of not being able to find anybody else. Many women cling to the old notion that a woman can change a husband, and *this* is reinforced by the codependent's general system of denial. Codependence, as I've seen repeatedly, operates with brutal efficiency to keep everyone it touches within its bounds. That is, until someone breaks the pattern.

Codependent husbands, however, are most able to leave their chemically dependent wives. This is because, quite simply, it is financially, socially, and psychologically easier. People are much quicker to condemn an alcoholic or drug-abusing wife than a husband: for some reason these habits are considered more "masculine" and therefore acceptable in a man. People are also quick to brand an addicted woman as an unfit wife or mother and to sympathize with a husband who wants to get out to save his children. By contrast, an addicted father usually has to become repeatedly and publicly violent or abusive or be involved in automobile accidents, fights, or arrests before people are likely to call him an "unfit" husband or father.

Then there are those marriages in which both partners are chemically dependent. Sometimes the marriage lasts through the addiction only to break up when one of them finally decides to get help. Getting help in a double-addicted marriage may be one of the most difficult things to do. But when it is necessary to leave the relationship altogether, guilt, concern, and a feeling of responsibility all weigh heavily on the one who tries to go. It seems like a callous, cruel, selfish form of abandonment. If one partner wants to recover, though, and the other doesn't, it may be the only way.

In another seemingly perplexing scenario, a codependent sometimes will break up the marriage *after* the dependent is well along in recovery. A patient of mine at the Outpatient Recovery Center recalls that her husband stuck by her through her long addiction to drugs, drugs that were first given to her for severe pain. "He stayed through my addiction, my detoxification, and through a horrible time when I had to have several operations without post-surgical pain relief. And then, just when I was finally really recovering, he divorced me."

This is most likely to happen if the codependent has done nothing about his or her own recovery. The codependent is suddenly without a role or an occupation; the dependent has now found a better source of help than drugs, but where does that leave the partner? Some codependents are jealous and bitter; after years of struggling, suddenly the dependent starts getting well and it's all thanks to the rehab personnel or the twelve-step group. As one wife said, "I can't stand him any more. All he does is go to meetings and come home and talk about AA." The codependent who isn't working on recovery may, without realizing it, be envious of the dependent who is. And, of course, codependents may suddenly be in a fix when they lose the handy excuse for everything that was wrong in the family.

Recovery brings out a lot of pent-up anger in *both* spouses. If an alcoholic woman was guilty, helpless, and subservient while she was still drinking, her husband may find her new self-sufficiency very hard to take. If a drug-addicted man used to come to his wife for comfort when he was sick and strung out, his wife may feel a terrible loss when she no longer has that "helpless little boy" to look after. Some codependents have sheepishly admitted that they hated losing the "upper hand" they had when the dependent was always drunk or stoned. If a wife wanted to buy a whole new wardrobe, for instance, all she had to do was wait till her husband was looped. When her husband stops drinking, her immediate response might be, "You were more fun when you were on the stuff."

It should begin to be clear by now that the best answer for everyone is for *both* dependents and codependents to recover. Remembering that a codependent cannot bring about a dependent's recovery, you might be wondering if there are nevertheless things a codependent *can* and *should* do to help the dependent.

The first answer is, tend to your own recovery. The second is, let your own recovery guide you to an understanding of the dependent's problems and behavior. It *is* harder for the dependent.

Patience will be needed in large quantities. When a family waits a long time for sobriety and it finally appears, everybody expects paradise to arrive with it. During the wait, especially if it has been very long, the family has probably come to blame all problems on the drink or the drugs. When they stop, everybody assumes the problems will stop. They won't. All families have problems; it's just that healthy families deal with them in healthier ways, and your family hasn't learned yet how to do this.

Furthermore, recovery has some rough spots for both dependents and codependents. Both will have to have some compassion, exercise some restraint, and keep the emotional antennae working—so you can detect when behavior is triggered by some hard part of recovery instead of plain bad temper or a negative attitude.

Learning again how to communicate and negotiate is another priority. A good marriage can be a powerful force for recovery;

a marriage in which communications have broken down, or never existed, can be a powerful negative influence. Marriages in which the partners are able to solve problems together are helpful; marriages in which the partners are rigid and stuck in their bad problem-solving habits, or in which there are *no* rules or methods for solving problems, create important barriers to recovery. In the ideal situation, a couple express their thoughts and feelings openly but are able to see each other's point of view and to empathize with the other person's problems. In too many families of alcoholics or addicts, the dependent person often gets loud and angry when problems are being discussed; the arguments end in violence or with the dependent person just walking out and leaving the argument hanging there like air pollution.

In fact, it is not unusual for couples with poor problem-solving tactics actually to get into a fight when *discussing* a recent argument. It's expected that people sometimes get angry at each other; but in recovery—or at any other time—it's what they do with the anger that counts.

Closeness is another part of marriage that has two opposing sides. It's healthy for couples to feel a warm closeness with each other; but too much closeness is not necessarily better than none. Couples can be so close and so identified with each other they can't see their own individuality, they begin to project their own feelings onto the other person, or they act as if they were "inside" the other person's mind. Such couples often tell each other what the other is feeling or thinking—no matter how wrong they might be. They say things like "You're just saying this doesn't bother you. You're really hurt but just won't admit it," or "You don't really want to take me to the movies; you just don't want to feel guilty about saying no." This is a form of control and it can lead to enormous frustration on the part of the person who's mind is being "read." Such comments are impossible to answer or refute. They might sound understanding, but they're really a subtle way of negating the other person's self. It's like saying, "You don't really exist; your feelings aren't valid; what counts is what *I* tell you." Such couples desperately need separate help on their recovery.

One of the most important problems in the recovery of both dependents and codependents is not being able to tell the difference between problems that were directly caused by the drinking or drug-taking, and problems that stem from basic emotional and psychological problems (including, for instance, the problems caused by your being the child of an alcoholic or addict). Many recovering dependents learn the essential lesson that removing the alcohol or drugs does not remove the kind of distorted attitudes and behavior that preceded the dependence and worsened during it. Recovering people refer to it as "stinking thinking" and know that it persists even when the drink and drug are removed. It takes time, and a lot of significant changes in attitudes, thoughts, and behavior by each individual in order to make significant changes in a marriage or other family relationships.

Treatment for Codependents

For codependents as for dependents, there are a variety of readily available kinds of help. Many rehabilitation centers, such as the Outpatient Recovery Center of Fair Oaks Hospital, offer concurrent but separate therapy for the partners or families of dependents.

Family programs at Fair Oaks begin before or while the dependent is in rehabilitation and continue for a minimum of three months afterward. Many programs actually offer residential care.

Presently, families are seen as addicted to the alcoholic or drug addict in much the same way the dependent is addicted to chemical substances. "The families have to be taught to find a new resource within themselves, to find a peer group, and to stop reacting to and attempting to control the alcoholic," according to my colleague Dr. Robert F. Stuckey, former medical director of the Alcohol Rehabilitation Unit at the hospital. "Teaching them this type of healthy selfishness is the only way to interrupt their addiction and their enabling role in the abnormal system." To return the rehabilitated dependent to an untreated family is to "seriously lower the probability of recovery for them all."

Treatment involves individual sessions and shared common experiences of recovery in group therapy centering around "here and now" feelings, to break the obsession with a painful past and what had been an uncertain future.

Alanon groups, based on the principals of Alcoholics Anonymous, can be tremendously helpful as an adjunct to rehabilitation center treatment and as aftercare. It is an interesting fact that many people who enter Alanon discover there that their problem is not just codependence but dependence, that their lives had become unmanageable not just because of "his drinking" or "her drug taking," but the codependent's own problems with chemical dependence—which had been overshadowed by the partner's more severe addiction. In the same way, many people who enter codependence programs or groups discover that they also suffer from what's known as the Adult Children of Alcoholics syndrome; many children of alcoholics or addicts may escape becoming alcoholics or addicts themselves but tend to marry chemically dependent partners. There are also groups that provide help for this illness.

Codependents may sometimes need additional individual psychotherapy, and in some cases it is helpful for a dependent and codependent couple to have marriage counseling as an adjunct to other therapy.

The significant point is that nobody needs to suffer and struggle alone with codependence. The help is there; all that is needed is to choose freedom and life over imprisonment and pain.

Children of Alcoholics

Looking at the problem of the children of alcoholics and drug users may require something like bifocals. You need to see the problems that your dependence has caused them; but at the same time, you should be trying to recognize the ill effects that having an alcoholic or drug-abusing parent has had on *you*. Many of the descriptions of your children's emotional problems and pain will also describe the problems and pain you have felt—but *probably didn't realize it at the time*. Many alcoholics and drug users are astonished when they recognize their childhood selves in their own children today.

The more you can learn about children of alcoholics and addicts, the more you will learn about yourself—and the more it will help both their recovery and yours.

At Fair Oaks Hospital, the Outpatient Recovery Center offers an intensive education and treatment program for adults who grew up in alcoholic families. By taking an objective look at his or her family of origin, each patient learns to identify feelings that require expression and behavior patterns that need to be changed. Repressed, "stuffed" feelings might include many of the following:

Shame	Hopelessness
Anger	Helplessness
Rage	Insecurity
Resentment	Inadequacy
Fear	Anxiety
Terror	Low self-esteem
Guilt	Fear of abandonment

Self-defeating behavior patterns might include these:

Denial	Blaming
Approval seeking	Self-criticism
Isolation	Difficulty trusting
Compulsions (about food, work, money, or sex)	Avoiding intimacy
Inappropriate relationships	Difficulty with authority
Controlling	Difficulty setting limits
Caretaking	Inability to make commitments
Perfectionism	Fear of failure
Procrastination	Repeating the victim role

No two children of the chemically dependent are alike, any more than any other two children are alike, or any two sets of parents are alike. Just as no attempt to define "the addictive personality" has ever met with universal agreement, no child can be made to fit a precisely defined picture of "the child of an alcoholic or addict." Yet all such children do grow up with certain very similar family patterns and influences, and so they do share many of the shame problems and personality patterns. Two things in particular are almost universal: these children grow up with shame, and they are taught to hide it. One adult child of an alcoholic parent spoke for almost all such families when he said, "In our family there were two rules. The first rule was: Never wash your dirty linen in public; never talk about family matters outside the house. As soon as you got the hang of that, you learned rule two: Never talk about it inside the house either."

Such children also grow up with sadness, which they also learn to hide, too. This rigidly imposed silence and denial leads them to develop rigid behavior patterns that prevent them from changing and growing—until they get help.

They also grow up not knowing the difference between love and need, between relationships with give-and-take and relationships in which one person always needs to be in control. Because they don't grow up learning healthy patterns of behavior, they have to invent ways of feeling as if they have some control over events, people, and their environment. These patterns of behavior develop into personality types which allow them to function in their sick families, but which prove self-destructive in the outside world.

Melody Beattie, in her landmark book, *Codependency* (Deerfield, Fla: Health Communications, 1988), presents a variety of names for these types; for example:

"The successfully, compulsively achieving *hero* . . . was the rallying point around which the family staked its claim that it was a normal, healthy, family." This is the one who got good grades, who lied for the parent when his or her employer called, who went to work at an early age to relieve the family's financial burden, who fixed things around the house and was "always there" when anybody in the family needed support.

"The hostile, rejecting *scapegoat* who shunned the family and acted out his feelings in an attempt to get attention from a system that was already spread too thin." This was the one who tried to keep a low profile but was always bawled out for the least transgression or became the excuse for quarrels between the parents or who was always compared unfavorably with the hero.

"The *lost child* withdrew from the emotional chaos of family life in a seemingly benign way, but in fact learned a cope-through-avoidance style which is devastating to the adult in terms of experiencing the richness of life." This one had no big ambitions but settled for the high school diploma or less and an undemanding job with no future and no possibility of personal distinction; who spent free time in his or her room or taking long walks; who avoided competitive sports or activities in school, and who tried to escape attention by getting neither superior grades nor failing marks.

"The *family mascot*, whose function was to provide comic relief for the family and learned to mask his most urgent communications ('love me, want me, accept me') with humor." This was the class cut-up, the mischievous one who did imitations or funny sound effects, and who never cried, never was sad—at least not in front of anyone else.

All of these children of alcoholics are cursed with low self-esteem, very little insight into their feelings and behavior, and a permanent sense of defeat; they feel that trying to change anything is hopeless. They tried to stop or reduce the parent's drinking, drug taking, fighting, and other destructive behavior, but they had no resources, nor did they have any idea of the unshakable principle that you cannot change the behavior of any other human being through direct action. Because they had no power over the chemical dependence, eventually they concluded they had no power over anything else, including themselves.

Among the many problems that confront such children, who have no resources for dealing successfully with them, are:

• Worrying about the health of the dependent parent.

• Being upset and angry about the unpredictable and inconsistent behavior of the dependent parent and the lack of support from the codependent parent, who is too busy trying to deal with the dependent parent to devote appropriate attention to the child.

• Worrying about fights and arguments between his or her parents.

• Being scared and upset by the violence or possibility of violence in the family.

• Being disappointed by broken promises and feeling unloved.

- Feeling responsible for his or her parents' dependence
  and other problems.

Children are often quite understandably confused about the cause of these problems. They may be too young to recognize alcoholism or drug abuse or they may have been taken in by the family's denial and the parents' regular reassurance that "there's nothing wrong." They may develop their own denial and try to find other excuses or reasons. They may blame themselves.

One daughter of an alcoholic mother, for example, was having problems with school phobia, feelings of unpopularity, and of being unattractive. When she talked to her mother about these problems during the daytime, her mother was sympathetic, responsive, and helpful. But in the evening, the mother came home from work, had her habitual drinks, became short-tempered, resentful, impatient, and unsympathetic. She would cut short her daughter's attempts to talk or would belittle her problems or answer in irrational, pointless ways. The mother's alcoholism had never been admitted; the father never spoke of it or appeared to recognize any problem. If questioned, the mother would answer sullenly that she was tired from work, cooking, taking care of the family, and so on. The daughter could not accept this answer; her mother was always "tired" at certain times, whether she had worked hard that day or not. So because the girl could see no other explanation, she concluded that her mother was tired of _her_, was sick of hearing _her_ problems, didn't care for _her_, and considered _her_ a nuisance. Sometimes the mother would become angry and abusive, and the daughter would beg her to explain "what I've done to make you so angry with me and hate me so much."

Although parents may attempt to cover up or to "protect" the children from the shameful knowledge of alcoholism or drug abuse, no amount of denial and lies can prevent children from knowing that something is wrong. Children are remarkably sensitive to their parents' tensions and moods; they can see their parents' actions, expressions, and attitudes. Parents can try to hide the truth about these things from their children, but they cannot prevent them from affecting the children. The children only become confused and insecure.

In the household of an alcoholic or drug abuser, family life is inconsistent, unpredictable, arbitrary, and chaotic. The child never knows whether the affected parent is going to be kind or cruel, at home or missing, whether the parent will remember promises or even remember anything said or done the day before. Parents don't have consistent rules: One day you can do a certain thing with impunity, but when you do the same thing the next day you get screamed at.

Children of alcoholics learn specific lessons from this. They learn to repress spontaneity, to first check things out to see if their parents are sober, and to shrug off disappointment. The absence of stability and the presence of dishonesty and denial lead the children of dependents to develop the first of many unhealthy characteristics and problems that they will carry with them into adulthood: distrust of self and others. Some of the other problems are:

Control and fear of the loss of control as a central issue in life: COAs have seen their parents lose control through drink or drugs; they have experienced the total inability to control that situation or anything else in family or personal life; they see the specter of chaos in all relationships in which they cannot exert control and in all feelings over which they lack control.

Avoidance of feelings and the conviction that having feelings (not just expressing them) is wrong and scary. The child's attempts to share or express feelings are brushed aside by the dependent parent who is too drunk or stoned to care, and by the codependent who is too absorbed in the dependent's problems to listen or respond. Because of the parent's commitment to denial, the child may be told such things as, "Don't ever say that to me. Don't even think it," or "How *dare* you disagree or talk back to me." The child learns first to hide feelings and then not to feel them. COAs also see how feelings are turned into action by a chemically dependent parent who becomes uninhibited and lets loose anger or even violence. Therefore, the child concludes, it is dangerous to have feelings because those feelings can become bad acts.

Most COAs who themselves become alcoholics or addicts say that in recovery one of the most important things you learn is that it is okay to have whatever feelings you have; what is important is *how you act on them*. "Once I accepted that it was okay to have feelings," says one adult COA, "I could make those feelings mine, and once they were mine I could do something with them—express them, use them, get rid of them, learn from them, whatever. But most of all, *feel* them." Many adult COAs recognize themselves in the joke about the man who never laughed or cried. He never married, never had a friend, never won or lost a race, never had anyone whose illness or death caused him to grieve. And when he died, the insurance company refused to pay on the grounds that he had never been alive.

Over-responsibility or misplaced guilt: This comes from the child so often having to take on responsibilities too big for his or her age. The child may also wrongly blame himself if the dependent parent runs out on the family or if something bad happens to a parent after the child has had angry thoughts or said, "I wish you were dead!" Children often confusedly think a parent drinks or take drugs because they have done something wrong or are "bad." They can't possibly know or understand that alcoholics drink and addicts take drugs because they have lost the ability to choose not to. They don't do it because of their problems; if that were true, everybody would be an alcoholic or an addict. They do it because they can't stop. If this is a difficult concept for so many adults to accept, it's not hard to see why a child would be painfully confused.

Ignoring one's own needs: In the diseased family, the disease comes first. All family life centers on this. The child's needs take second place to the need for protection of the chemically dependent person, protection of the family secret, solving financial problems, and all the other complications of codependent family life. The child begins to assume that he doesn't have the right to have needs and certainly doesn't have any reason to expect those needs will be met. Such children grow up into people who always say "Never mind about *me*. Whatever's best for you."

Dissociation: Adult COAs often don't make the connection between a feeling and the situation that gives rise to that feeling. "I'm depressed and I don't have any idea why." They may also express feelings inappropriately; laughing nervously at sad or frightening situations; crying for no reason or because they are angry, not sad. They often appear expressionless even when they are having a powerful feeling, a phenomenon that psychologists call "flattened affect," like someone who is in a trance.

Adrenaline "addiction": Some children become so used to the wild roller-coaster life of the dependent family that they are uncomfortable or feel at a loss when nothing exciting or threatening is happening. These people may take up dangerous sports or may get their adrenaline jolts in more subtle ways, such as inventing crises or maneuvering their way into a crisis, or postponing things to the last minute so they can make a mad dash to the deadline.

Low self-esteem is the net result of all of these problems and feelings. It comes from these children learning not to trust themselves, from not knowing their own feelings. It comes from having an all-or-nothing way of looking at things—if it's not perfect then they've failed. It comes from always having to subjugate their needs, from living in a world where they believe, and where they have been made to believe, that they are the cause of the family's problems. Since such children have a difficult time seeing themselves as valuable or worthwhile people, they have a difficult time realizing their right to be treated well, to set limits on what they will or will not do, on what they will or will not tolerate. This creates an adult who lacks a sense of personal identity.

The Problems of ACOAs

Wayne Kritsberg, in his book *The Adult Children of Alcoholics Syndrome,* sums up the problems of the adult COA as follows:

- Emotional: fear, anger, hurt, resentment, distrust, loneliness, sadness, shame, guilt, numbness.

- Mental: thinking in absolutes, lack of information, compulsive thinking, indecision, learning disabilities, confusion, hypervigilance.

- Physical: tense shoulders, lower back pain, sexual dysfunction, gastrointestinal disorders, sleep problems, allergies.

- Behavioral: crisis-oriented living, manipulative behavior, intimacy problems, inability to have fun, trying to fit in, compulsive-addictive disorders.

Among the compulsive addictive illnesses that are common among COAs are the eating disorders anorexia and bulimia. Experts have noted that the personality characteristics common to children with eating disorders are virtually identical to those of children of alcoholics or addicts. This, of course, does not mean that all people with eating disorders have alcoholic or addicted parents, merely that the kind of dysfunction that occurs in codependent families is likely to produce an eating disorder in a susceptible child, and that this kind of dysfunction can also be found in families that are "sick" for reasons other than alcoholism or drug addiction. These families also have children with eating disorders.

It's also been found that recovery for a child with an eating disorder can be made easier and more rapid when the dependent parent begins to recover, and that eating disorders are much harder to treat if the parent remains dependent.

Children of alcoholics and addicts, like codependent wives and husbands, learn survival strategies, not good coping techniques. It's like learning to type with two fingers. With enough practice, you can type. But you type very slowly, you make mistakes, and you have to keep looking at the keys, then at what you're typing, then back again. It can get the job done, but not very well, and it takes a lot of effort.

So children of the chemically dependent enter adulthood coping with life in the same ways that "worked" when they were children. Later, they discover that what worked in childhood does not serve them well in adult life. But, if we do not know any alternatives, we struggle vainly with the same old strategies we used in childhood.

In adulthood, such children tend to be overly serious, overly self-reliant, unable to trust, unable to cooperate, unable to relax, and always needing to be in control of every situation. This is a burden to them even if they escape the alcoholism or drug addiction themselves. Or perhaps they find their release by imitating their parent—and taking to drink or drugs. Over and over in twelve-step meetings you hear this admission: "I'm such a controlling person. I always have to run things."

COA Recovery

Recovery programs or sources of help for COAs range from concurrent family therapy in a rehabilitation unit to psychotherapy for children too young for group work, to Alateen, Alanon, and Adult Children of Alcoholics groups.

Recovery for adult COAs, like recovery for everybody else involved—dependent or codependent—must begin with recognition. Adults who have been the children of the chemically dependent may be just as reluctant as dependents are to give up their habitual rules of coping. They have to be convinced, first of all, that this is what is causing them so much trouble in life. Second, they have to be convinced that the effort of recovering is worth it and is less painful than not recovering. Finally, they have to accept that seeking treatment doesn't constitute disloyalty to the dependent parent or parents. Once this recognition has taken place, the rewards are great: adult COAs can understand and realistically assess what happened in the past, work through the anger and resentment they feel toward the parent who caused all this pain, free themselves of confusion, guilt, and misplaced self-hatred, and look forward to the future with optimism, not with fear.

When the child of a chemically dependent parent finally comes to recognize that he or she has a problem that is attributable to parental alcoholism and seeks help, their instinct often is to share the "good news" with the rest of the family. They want to let everybody know their great discovery and the freedom and recovery this knowledge seems to promise. Restraint is the rule here. Siblings and other family members may not want to know about it. They may deny it, they may be angry because of the threat to their entrenched denial and their habitual role behaviors, or they may resent the one who is trying to break out of the prison they are not yet able to confront. They may suggest that the one seeking recovery is a little crazy and is trying to shift the blame for the craziness onto the parent or parents. At the moment these other people can't be helped because they are not ready and are still too heavily engaged in denial. Nor is their recovery the responsibility of the child who *is* trying to recover. That person's sole responsibility and duty at the moment is to his or her own recovery. If you want to share this gift of recovery with someone else, choose a best friend or better still, other ACOAs who are also recovering.

This matter of sharing—both the good and the bad—is an important part of relearning the trust you lost as the child of a chemical dependent. It can't be done instantly; it must be done step by step. You might begin with a small confidence and see how the other person reacts. If they turn away, try someone else, until you receive encouragement. One of the best ways to learn trust and to discover that it is not only safe but very healthy and satisfying to be honest about yourself is to go to group programs such as Alanon and see how other people do it. It's okay to sit in the back of the room at first and just listen. After a while, move up front and speak when your turn comes. It may feel uncomfortable at first, but it will be a great relief when you get used to it.

Some special words to teenagers who have just discovered they are children of alcoholics or addicts: Life is especially complicated for you because the anger and resentment you feel toward your alcoholic or addict parent (or parents) is compounded by the natural rebellion all young people feel toward their parents at this age. It will probably be impossible for you to separate these two things; it may not be necessary.

What *is* essential is that you recognize and accept your feelings as the natural result of your situation and get help in dealing with them. You may find it difficult to make this decision. One of the problems in any adolescence is that while you're doing the work that is appropriate to this stage of growing up—that is, transferring your focus from parents and family to peers and the outside world—you also are feeling a little guilty or even very guilty for turning away from your family. You may feel even more guilty if the family you are turning away from is a family in trouble. You feel like the usual rat leaving the usual sinking ship. This is pretty much to be expected, and teenagers who don't have a chemically dependent parent manage to deal with the guilt, to accomplish the natural separation from home at the natural time, and even to be reconciled with their parents after it's over. For you, suffering through the guilt until it goes away with time is particularly dangerous. You need help coping with your family, if you want to have a healthy development and a healthy adulthood. Look at it this way: your parent or parents aren't doing their job for you, which is to encourage your growth and independence and help you make this healthy transition from child to grown-up. They are incapable of it while they're on drink or drugs, so you have to find help elsewhere. There is no reason to feel guilty; it isn't your fault that your parents have this problem. (It isn't really theirs, either, but it may be a long time before you can accept that.) And in the long run, you'll be doing them a favor as well as doing yourself one. By seeking help for yourself, you may even open their eyes to their own need for help.

Your life will be even more complicated if, like an unfortunately large number of young people, you have followed your parents' path to alcoholism or addiction. You need a lot of help. If you're smart enough or desperate enough to seek it, you will probably be told you are "lucky" that you are trying to overcome your dependence so early in your life, compared to those adults who have wasted years and years in dependence and have lost jobs, lost their families, gone to jail, ruined their health, and suffered overwhelming guilt over what they have done to their spouse and their children. Unless you are a remarkably mature young person, your response to this is, "That's a lot of junk. Why should I feel lucky? What's so lucky about being stuck with alcoholism or addiction at my age? Why me?"

You're angry. You think it's unfair to be stuck with this affliction, which you did nothing to cause. You're mad because you've been told that alcoholism and addiction are *for life*, and if you want to save yourself, you have to accept the fact that you can *never* have one drink or one drug or go on Saturday-night binges with your friends who can drink or do drugs and get by with it (although a lot of them are going to discover after a while that they can't get by with it either. You just found it out sooner). You're mad because you're going to miss all the fun.

Unfortunately, you're also not going to want to hear it when people tell you you're not going to miss any fun, you're just going to miss a lot of heartache and misery. Most teenagers find it impossible to accept the experience of older people. It is a sad fact—and one that frustrates most parents out of their minds when their children reach adolescence—that some experience can't be handed down like the family silverware. There are things you just have to learn for yourself by going through your own tough times. That's okay when it comes to things like having your heart broken or flunking a course because you didn't study. But learning about drink and drugs the hard way can cost too much. It can destroy you. So if you won't listen to adults and you don't dare learn it by experience, what's your alternative?

There's one good possibility, and if you're willing to just give it a try, it works. You can learn it from people your own age or people just a few years older who are going through it or have been through it. Find an Alanon/Alateen group (see lists at the end of this book or search the yellow pages). Find an AA or NA group with a lot of young members. (There are plenty of them. Call AA and ask if there are any groups that meet at the local high school, or just go to any AA meeting, find somebody your age, and ask them if there's a younger group anywhere.) You're probably not going to want to do this, unless you are driven to it by unmanageable and intolerable pain—and even then your natural rebelliousness may make you too stubborn to do it. Think of it as a new way to meet guys or girls.

Go to a few meetings. Don't just go to one and say, "Yuck." Try again until you really begin to get the gist of what's going on; it may not be all that obvious the first time. Or try other groups until you find one in which you feel comfortable. You'll be surprised how many groups there are for teenagers, and how much you'll have in common. In fact, you'll probably learn something strange: you are not unique. Everybody there knows what you've been through and what you're going through, and most of all, *they care about you and want to help*. That should feel good after all the time you've spent in a family that didn't seem to give a damn.

The recovering child of an alcoholic or addict, whether teenager or adult, will need patience. Like the addict, you will think that discovering your problem and deciding to attack it will open the door to an immediate transformation of your life; all problems solved, all conflict resolved, all pain relieved. It doesn't work that way. You will still have problems, you will still make mistakes, you will still fall into some of the old traps—playing a role, protecting others, taking on responsibilities that are not yours. Remind yourself regularly that it is all right to make mistakes as long as your general progress is forward, not backward. You are not seeking perfection; you are striving for improvement.

If you get discouraged, take out a pencil and paper and write down all the changes you have noticed, however small. Don't let yourself lose sight of the difference between where you are and where you were when you started.

On the other hand, you may get scared when things start going really well all the time. You may wonder when the bubble is going to burst, or you may even start looking for trouble. You might ask yourself when you are going to be punished for being too contented, or you may figure that eventually you are going to have to pay for this new satisfaction with yourself and your life. "You have already paid the price—and an exorbitant fee it was."

And of course, things are *not* always going to be uniformly great. Recovery is not paradise; it is normal, normal life with all the normal difficulties. Don't try to do it all at once; a journey consists of many single steps. But every step makes the next one easier.

7

INTIMACY AND SEXUALITY

WHEN WE TALK ABOUT RECOVERY WE ARE TALKING NOT JUST about abstinence but recovery in a whole sense—as it touches on functioning in all areas of life, all attitudes and feelings, and in particular about your sense of identity, self-esteem, and wholeness as a human being. A central issue must be relationships with others, particularly the closest and most intimate relationship with a partner, including the sexual relationship.

Because chemical dependence eats away at all relationships, it is bound to damage or even destroy this most fundamental of all relationships. When honesty, trust, openness, and compassion have eroded away, the emotional intimacy essential to good sexual relationships also dies. Sexual and emotional recovery between partners is a matter of reforging the links of intimacy and reviving the respect and caring that leads to and characterizes a healthy sexual union.

Closely tied into the emotional and psychological problems of dependence and codependence are some serious physical effects. Some of these are not only destructive of sex during dependence, they may linger well into the recovery period, complicating efforts to repair the damage that dependence has done to the partnership. Thus, although the emotional relationship is the most important victim of chemical dependence and the one requiring the most work and good will during recovery, the physical aspects need to be known, understood, and dealt with.

The Physical Costs

Chief among these are anorgasmia or inability to achieve orgasm (which used to be called frigidity), and erectile dysfunction (previously called impotence).

Anorgasmia is fairly common among chemically dependent women as well as among the partners of chemically dependent men. Loss of sexual interest and inability to experience sexual pleasure are, to begin with, a direct result of the physical and biochemical effects of alcohol and drugs. Your body just doesn't work the way it did; you are probably suffering from poor nutrition, poor sleep, and lack of exercise along with the direct effects of drink or drugs, including depletion of the chemicals necessary to healthy intellectual and emotional function. Many other things contribute to or complicate the physical problem. Among dependent women these include guilt, reduced sexual drive due to the depressant effect of alcohol or drugs, and fear of the loss of control—one of the most important issues in chemical dependence. Dependents live with and live on the fantasy that they can control their drinking or drugging, so they must also fight a constant battle to be in control of other parts of their lives. This can be especially threatening to women, for whom the sexual act involves a kind of surrender. Women also may become less inhibited while drinking or taking drugs and afterward feel guilt and fear over having been too free or abandoned, of being an "object" or "too loose." Women today face many conflicts about their sexuality and their sexual behavior;

the old stereotyped roles still haunt them even while they are being told they no longer have to play them. For women who are emotionally confused and insecure because of their dependence or codependence, the ambiguity and the challenge of this situation can be extremely unsettling. Codependent women who remain in a subservient sexual relationship and who begin to find intercourse intolerable may be paralyzed by guilt.

Erectile dysfunction is a problem in a large percentage of alcoholics and drug abusers—despite the folklore about the power of various chemicals to enhance sexual performance and pleasure. Cocaine, in particular, is associated with several myths that serve to glamorize its use, especially myths about its effectiveness as a sort of sexual supervitamin pill. Cocaine intoxication has been rumored to increase libido, prolong intercourse, facilitate multiple erections, produce more intense orgasms, and even produce spontaneous ejaculation. While there is some truth to these tales, the reality doesn't begin to approach the epic proportions of stories spread by cocaine users. And unfortunately, whatever positive effect cocaine may have is limited to acute use; among chronic users, the actual sexual low is as low as the reputed sexual high is high. Erectile dysfunction is a common effect of prolonged cocaine use just as it is for alcohol or drugs other than cocaine; heroin, for example, which appears to cause dysfunction in up to 50 percent of chronic users. It is another result of the biochemical imbalance and the depletion of certain neurotransmitters (notably dopamine and norepinephrine) caused by chemical abuse, along with reduced sex hormone levels in many cases.

The Psychological Costs

The physical problem carries with it a heavy psychological toll. The loss of potency strikes hard at the self-esteem of chemical dependents whose self-esteem is already in jeopardy. Recovering alcoholics who are discouraged about their sexual competence often resume drinking because of the emotional pain regarding their masculinity. During early recovery, chemically dependent people may be surprised by continued dysfunction because they may assume that it was simply a result of being drunk or drugged. In fact, erectile difficulty may persist because of a low testosterone level, which doesn't correct itself immediately. It can take as long as twelve weeks after the beginning of abstinence for the physical causes of dysfunction to be reversed.

In both addicts and their partners, past failures and the anxiety about performance may well be the major stumbling block to a satisfying sexual relationship. The great emphasis placed on sexual performance in this culture, and its subsequent anxiety, makes life even more difficult for a recovering chemically dependent/codependent person who is suffering from sexual dysfunction.

Sexual partners suffer as well, not only because of the loss of intimacy and sexual satisfaction, but because these also represent a blow to self-esteem. Many codependent women report feeling sexually inferior and inadequate because they still believe at some level they are responsible for their husbands' problems and if they were better women their husbands would have erections.

Since the sexual relationship plays such a central role in most marriages or partnerships, some partners keep trying even when intimacy is practically gone or when they are handicapped by impotence or anorgasmia; they think if they can keep on being loving in bed, everything will be okay. This is bound to lead to disappointment. The physical and emotional barriers to sexual fulfillment will only feed disappointment and resentment, and attempts to achieve sexual intimacy cannot lead to or substitute for the emotional intimacy that is absolutely required for a healthy sexual relationship. The only way back is through the recovery of both dependent and codependent and the discovery of a new basis for love and sex.

Of course, whatever happens during recovery is going to be influenced powerfully by what happened emotionally and psychologically during the period of dependence. Aside from the physical barriers to satisfactory sex, dependents and codependents also suffer seriously from low self-esteem during active addiction. Chemical dependence is "an assault on one's value system" that leads both partners to be confused and to question their very deepest nature. "How could I let this happen to me?" they ask. "I must be a rotten human being to be an alcoholic (or addict)," "I must not have any character at all to let my life be taken over by an alcoholic (or addict)." It is extremely difficult, if not impossible, to love another person if you do not love yourself.

Just to compound these difficulties, many chemically dependent people grew up as children of alcoholics or addicts and had a very precarious notion, if any, of how to have a healthy emotional and sexual life to begin with. Many children of alcoholics/addicts grow up believing that sex is all they have to share with someone else, or is all that someone else ever wants from them. Some mistakenly believe that by "giving themselves" in sex they have achieved real intimacy and communion. Such people, already prone to be confused about most of their feelings, have no real idea about the difference between sex and intimacy, nor do they understand that you can have one without the other but it's not a very satisfactory arrangement.

Some chemically dependent people may suffer the added burden of guilt over extramarital affairs they've had while drinking or taking drugs and guilt over the lying and deceit that naturally goes with this behavior. They know these are things they would not have done otherwise, that they are outside their true characters and values, and this lowers their self-esteem further. They may begin to feel unworthy of a healthy sexual relationship. What the unfaithful partner may overlook is that the other partner (as in so many other aspects of their lives) may be "enabling" the unfaithfulness as part of their "marytr" role or as a way of avoiding an intimacy they now find repugnant. Both the dependent's guilt and the partner's enabling must be recognized and dealt with.

Women who have extramarital affairs seem to be more badly damaged by it than men are, since there is a greater stigma attached to female unfaithfulness and to female alcoholism or addiction. Women also feel they have to "live down" the erroneous but widespread belief that drink or drugs automatically makes them more promiscuous.

Some sexually dysfunctional women use their drinking or drugging in the hope of feeling feminine, sexually aroused, and stimulated when they can't face the fact that they aren't really capable of feeling anything at all. Then they use drink or drugs to relieve their anxieties about their sexual inadequacy. Other women submit to sexual advances or activities that they would resist if they had any self-respect left. Their guilt and shame make them feel they have no right to set limits or to determine what behavior is acceptable to them and what is not.

Partners can easily be sexually turned off by a drink or drug habit. The partner may reek of alcohol or may be less careful about personal appearance and cleanliness. A once enthusiastic and responsive woman may become lethargic and indifferent when she is using chemicals. A once tender and gentle lover may become insensitive or even brutal. Some men have been brought up in what could be called "rough-tough" families in which gender roles fit old stereotypes: macho male and passive female. These families tend not only to act tough but also to talk tough: "Get your butt out of that chair and let your mother sit down!" Such men may in fact be uncertain about their own sexuality or dare not reveal any tenderness or gentleness because they assume it will be seen as evidence of homosexuality. Sexual relationships with such men can be difficult in normal circumstances, and when chemical dependence enters the situation the roughness can escalate into physical abuse or violence. Women from such families likewise have problems with their sexual identity and are often lacking in self-respect; when they become dependent or codependent they may become even more abject,

---

thus inviting more scorn or more abuse from their partners.

The dependent one is quite likely to shift the blame for sexual problems onto the codependent, who probably already feels guilty about not being as responsive or easily aroused as before.

Physical attraction and the sexual relationship may remain intact for a while after dependence begins. Both partners may try harder or will convince themselves that things are still fine as the denial of the dependence spreads out into denial of other difficulties. As the partners begin to move away from each other emotionally and the barriers to communication build up, they may desperately look to sex for a common meeting place and a chance to share. Sex may become not only the best but the only way to make up after a violent quarrel. Someone who considers sex a fundamental way of expressing love may try (at least during sober or drug-free times) to offer it as an apology or a way of making up for not providing the warmth, affection, and approval the partner used to get from the relationship. The alcoholic or addict who thinks sex brings forgiveness for every wrong may find his partner withholding sex because he or she doesn't want to forgive.

Gradually the interest in physical intimacy weakens and the rewards become less compelling than the difficulties and anxieties. The codependent partner becomes wary and needs to avoid the vulnerability he or she feels when a drunk or drugged partner wants to have sex. The physical act itself becomes more mechanical and less pleasurable as the emotions become less and less involved. The talk or play or other ways a couple used to engage in as a way of leading into the physical act is reduced or even omitted entirely. As the feeling of understanding and being understood wanes or disappears entirely, the nondependent partner begins to feel like a nonperson, and the chemically dependent partner feels the distance and resents it. The codependent partner may begin to withhold sex as a punishment or as a way of pressuring the dependent partner to get straight.

Friendship is lost. Lovers become adversaries. Sex becomes a battleground or no-man's-land. And of course, nobody is capable of talking about it. Angry words and recriminations on both sides replace any attempt at revealing true feelings or trying to uncover the partner's true feelings.

Eventually, the partners become more consumed by their own personal fears, anguish, and isolation, even while they are still united by their dependence. At this point, many partners give up sex. Then comes the revolutionary change: abstinence and the beginning of recovery for partners whose relationship has deteriorated to the point where sex is either unpleasant, disappointing, or absent entirely. Expectations are raised in all areas of their lives, including the sexual. Early in recovery, the dependent partner may still be suffering reduced sexual drive and other physical barriers to sex. The codependent may still be too turned off, too resentful, or just too worn down to want to resume a physical relationship. But eventually, as other aspects of their lives begin to improve, their interest in resuming a sexual life may also revive.

Unfortunately, they may assume that this will simply be a natural outcome of abstinence and recovery and that one day soon, they will find themselves physically reunited as a matter of course. When the drinking or drugging goes away, the sex comes back, they think.

It doesn't happen like that. Many of the things that stood in the way of sex during dependence do diminish or disappear; the physical sloppiness, the violence, the lies and deception, the unfaithfulness. The other obstacles to intimacy and sex are not so easily removed.

Look at what has been lost: the most fundamental needs in a human relationship—trust, honesty, respect, concern, understanding. These are things that require good will and hard work even in a partnership that is not beset with all the ills of chemical dependence. These are things that build slowly in any partnership and that must be nurtured throughout the lifetime of that partnership. In a chemically dependent partnership, they have been subject to deadly blows from which they are not likely to recover overnight. Sometimes they never do.

Recovery requires dedication and work on both sides. In fact, at the very beginning the partners may have to decide on whether they are looking for the same things and are equally willing to strive for those things. You are not the same two people you were before the dependence began or before it destroyed so much of your lives. You can't go back to where you were *then*; you have to start from where you are *now*.

The Road Back

All of the things you have to learn and do will require help from a therapist, from a rehabilitation aftercare program, and especially from twelve-step group participation by *both* of you. Healing a desperately injured relationship is no job for do-it-yourself doctors, nor should it be based solely on the guidance and advice of well-meaning friends or relatives, who lack the needed expertise and who may have their own biases and agendas. In fact, while you may ask such people for their support and patience, you should politely make it clear from the outset that you are getting the guidance you need from a professional or a group, and that advice from others might conflict with that guidance and ultimately confuse you.

The first essential to this aspect of your recovery is patience. When you take the tremendous step of giving up your chemical and starting on the work of recovery, you will want everything to happen immediately. You will probably expect your partner to recognize instantly that things are going to be different, and you will assume that he or she will jump at the chance to put things right again. You are most likely to be disappointed in this, because you need time for the physical effects of your chemical dependence to be corrected, and you both need time to heal the emotional wounds. The reunion, both emotional and physical, is going to have to happen step by step rather than in one leap. Try to make each step an adventure, a source of pleasure in itself, and you won't worry so much about the next step or how far you have to travel to get to your destination. You can make getting there half the fun. The idea is to do some simple, basic, even practical things that will bring with them deeper and more far-reaching rewards. For example, long before you resume full sexual relations with your partner, you have to begin to talk. This is the most important way in which you are going to restore communications, closeness, and honesty, the best way you can learn each other's hurts and needs and problems so you can help each other to experience them, express them, and deal with them.

The honesty required for good relationships, including good sexual relationships, is extremely difficult for recovering chemical dependents, for whom lying and dishonesty have become a way of life. An unquestionably good way to achieve honesty is by active participation in AA, NA, CA, or codependent groups such as Alanon or Adult Children of Alcoholics. Attending a few meetings and hearing the candor and openness of other people talking about their experiences, their pain, and their growth make it clear that this is a *safe* place in which to talk, a place where no judgments are made, where admission of your worst faults is met with approval for the honesty rather than disapproval of the fault, and where all revelations and remarks are received with acceptance and affection. Once you learn to tell the truth in a safe place, it is easier to take the risk of telling the truth outside. The other lesson to be learned from speaking up at twelve-step meetings is that letting go of a secret and letting out your thoughts and feelings relieves pain and releases you from a great burden. Beginning to talk with your partner doesn't have to be, in fact shouldn't be, a serious and formal matter, with the two of you facing each other to "thrash things out." Instead, start talking about *anything* except sex or even "us." If you think about it, you will realize that it has probably been a long time since you actually had any conversation with your partner. Go to a movie, the theater, or a sports event. Talk about your reaction or your opinion, and ask your partner's opinion or reaction. Does the movie or event make you happy or angry or confused? Do you identify with any of the characters or players? Does it stir up your childhood dream of being an actor, a ballet dancer, a quarterback? Does it remind you of anything, especially something that perhaps you both shared when you were still sharing anything? Relax and let your thoughts free-associate. Talk about yourself; let out a secret. This may sound self-centered and all wrong under the circumstances, but it isn't. It's a way of saying that you want to share yourself with your partner again, instead of locking yourself away in drink or drugs.

Of course, talking about yourself is only the opener; it is an invitation to your partner to do the same. It's the first step in the wonderful game of "getting to know you," which is what you and your partner have to do all over again—only this time with honesty and trust. Stop worrying so much about making a good impression or only showing your best side, and in particular don't try to be what you think your partner wants you to be. Be yourself, even if you are still a little confused about who you are.

Along with talk that's intended to open up communications about feelings, needs, and desires, it's important to learn again to talk about things that require cooperation and joint decisions, beginning with small practical matters. Chances are you and your partner had reached a point where you couldn't agree on the most trivial decisions—what movie to see, whether to go to your cousin's wedding. Beginning again to discuss—not argue about—the everyday details of your life together will also open up a path to the bigger aspects of your life together, such as sex.

Next, make some promises, and *keep* them. Choose some area that used to be a source of irritation or argument between you, as long as this is a manageable area and not something massive or unforgivable. Avoid "I'll never look at another woman again." This is too sweeping a promise. Try something within easy range. For example, if you were always late when you were supposed to be somewhere or go somewhere with your partner, try *just once* to be on time. Then try it again. You can pick any small source of irritation, from forgetting to enter amounts in the checkbook to using up the last of the toilet paper and not putting another roll on. Making promises about such matters and keeping them will be a beginning toward earning back lost trust. One of the most visible and convincing ways of restoring trust and demonstrating your determination to keep your promise of recovery is simply being faithful in your commitment to attending aftercare counseling sessions or frequent, regular twelve-step meetings.

Inventories have proved to be an enormously useful tool in twelve-step programs, and they can help in getting your sexual life back to normal, too.

Taking inventory is a way of coming to know yourself, to help you gain knowledge that helps you not to repeat the behaviors that caused you to feel guilt and anxiety or that messed up your relationships with other people. A sexual inventory can do much the same thing. It will help you to know yourself sexually with more honesty than you allowed yourself before, and can reveal which areas of your sexual and emotional life with your partner were caused by your chemical dependence and which were due to basic differences or flaws in your relationship. It can also lead you to recognize that what is acceptable sexual behavior for one person may not be acceptable for another, and some may in fact be a threat to sobriety. People are no more identical in their sexual values than in any other way.

First by yourself, and then with your partner, make an inventory of things that you used to do to hurt your partner, to sabotage good sex, to build up walls. Were you too quick to criticize? Did you pay attention to your partner's needs? For example, if one of you wanted to talk before or after sex and the other one didn't, did you always have it your way? If you wanted sex and your partner didn't, how did you react? Did you try to understand why, did you make any attempt to ease or win your partner into the right mood, or did you just get

mad and sulk or yell? Besides trying to empathize and understand your partner's feelings and needs, did you try to reveal
yours, or did you think it was your partner's duty to figure it
out? When people tell each other their needs, it's much easier
for the other person to respond or to say honestly, "I just can't
do that. But maybe we could compromise and do this, instead."
When people are silent about their feelings—including what they
want from another person—it closes the door to intimacy. It
says, "I don't care enough about this relationship, or I don't
trust you enough, to open myself up to you and tell you my
secrets." It also says, "I don't want to know your secrets. That's
why I won't tell you mine."

Taking inventory, by definition, always means counting up
not only what stock you lack but also what stock you have on
hand. So an "intimacy inventory" means not just checking out
the bad spots in your behavior and your relationship, but the
assets as well. What did you do and what can you do to bring
on a warm response rather than a big chill? What gave your
partner (and therefore *you*) pleasure? This doesn't mean sacri-
fices—they never do anybody any good or give anybody any
pleasure, neither the giver nor the receiver. It means, for example, "Did you love to cook and he loved to eat?" "Did she
love to get presents and you were proud to be able to give them
and pleased to see her enjoy them?" "What kind of nonsexual
intimacies usually preceded sex when things were still healthy
between you?" If you take a little time and thought over an
inventory, especially if you write it down, it will reap enormous
rewards for both of you.

At first, you may feel you're doing all the work. This seems
fair; after all, it was *your* chemical dependence that got you into
this fix in the first place. Taking inventory and telling your
partner what you are doing is a loud and clear signal of good
intentions, and asking your partner to join the exercise is a signal
that you want to be together again in everything.

Any cause of discord or conflict of needs causes more trouble
for a dependent partnership or for recovering partners than it

would for others. One such troublesome issue involves out-of-the-ordinary sexual practices. Sex therapists and other experts generally state that no sexual practice should be considered abnormal as long as it is acceptable to both partners. The problem is that quite often one partner will agree to a distasteful sexual activity just in order to please the other partner. Sometimes the reluctant partner becomes accustomed to the practice and even finds it enjoyable. More often, the reluctant partner becomes more repulsed and more unwilling and either calls a halt to the practice or continues it and slowly but inevitably builds up a serious reservoir of resentment. That can damage any relationship but can totally destroy one already weakened by the problems of chemical dependence. If the dependent is the reluctant partner, he or she may continue to give in to the partner's demands out of guilt, becoming more and more resentful, or may angrily refuse to participate when drunk or drugged. (Eventually the dependence may bring an end to this practice along with all sexual activity, but not before creating a major cause of dissension, hurt, and anger.) If the codependent is the unwilling partner, he or she is likely to add this to all the other sources of resentment and hostility that come with codependence. In either case the unwilling partner will probably accumulate a heavy burden of shame, which only exaggerates the low self-esteem that is so typical of both dependents and codependents.

This problem will require a lot of work, a lot of help, and a tremendous amount of good will. How much one's ego is involved in having a partner agree to all wishes will be an issue; so will the power struggle that all couples engage in to some degree and dependent couples to a really unhealthy extent. Each partner needs to ask and answer some critical questions: Is my need for this activity worth the pain it causes my partner? Does my reluctance to satisfy my partner in this way reflect moral or personal reluctance or is it a way of withholding myself to punish my partner? Is this just a difference in attitude that reflects our religions or the way we were brought up? Or is there a real

---

fundamental problem here involving mastery and subservience? This is an area where professional guidance may be required.

This is also an area in which listening, understanding, caring, and especially respect play a powerful role.

Respect, in fact, is really the name of the game in intimacy and sexuality—and is what becomes lost or buried when chemical dependence starts messing up a marriage or partnership. As recovering partners slowly regain their self-respect, however, they are much better able to relearn respect for each other. Some of it will come naturally as part of your efforts to communicate and understand each other. Some of it can be helped alone by the same kind of inventory taking that's useful in other parts of recovery. You can make a mental or written list of the things you respected in yourself and your partner when you first learned to love and care about each other. See how many are left; nourish those, and work on rediscovering or reinstating the ones that disappeared with drink and drugs.

What happens when your needs conflict so strongly that there doesn't seem to be any way to solve the problem? First of all— with professional help—you need to learn how to resolve conflicts without fighting. A big part of this is knowing when to keep your mouth shut and *listen*. One reason most arguments never resolve anything is that the combatants are only interested in saying, or shouting, what *they* want to say. Nobody is listening. Another reason is that men and women tend to fight with different styles, by different rules. For example, when an argument reaches a certain point of no return, and you both begin to repeat the same things, or when you begin to argue about the argument ("No, I didn't say that, I said so and so; then *you* said so and so), men in general have a tendency to walk away from it. "I don't want to discuss this anymore," or "There's no point trying to talk to you!" are typical argument-enders for men. Women, on the other hand, in general want to continue the argument until it reaches a resolution or just dies of exhaustion. Professional counselors can teach techniques that allow discussions or arguments to come to some closure or to be constructively resolved.

Compromise, of course, is always a good standby, although many people seem to think compromise is the same as selling out—or that it means "You want this and I want that, so we compromise and do what neither one of us wants to do." It doesn't have to be. For example: He likes sex in the morning but she's one of those people who are slow to wake up; she doesn't feel human until she's had coffee. She likes it at night, but usually he's too exhausted from work to enjoy it as much. A bad bargain would be to take turns, so each one gets first choice sometime— but whenever one partner has first choice, the other hates it. How about making the unattractive choice more attractive? Bring her breakfast in bed. That not only gives her time to wake up a little, it makes her feel you really care and want to please her. If he's tired at night, don't nag about his helping you with dinner dishes or other chores; don't start talking about unpleasant subjects such as the bank balance; don't act as if you automatically expect sex or have a "right" to sex when you get in bed. Let him relax after dinner or give him a chance to let off steam about the unpleasant things that happened to him at work. Encourage him to get some fatigue-fighting exercise such as a walk or a bike ride or shooting baskets with his friends. Give him a back rub or an all-over massage. It will not only fight his tiredness but make him feel pampered and in a much more loving mood.

Or how about sex in the afternoon? It's not only a compromise, it's something new and different and therefore potentially fun or exciting.

Nobody can give you a script that tells you in detail how to handle every argument or conflict of needs. The idea is to accept some basic points and adapt each situation to them. The basic point here is recognizing your partner's feelings as well as your own, respecting each other's needs, working toward solutions that make *both* of you winners rather than only one of you or neither of you.

One thing that may give you trouble with all this at first is just recognizing your own feelings. Chemically dependent people become so habituated to denying or dulling their feelings with drink or drugs that eventually they either stop feeling or don't know what they're feeling when they feel it. Recovering people usually find it necessary, and helpful, to stop and think about their feelings, to say to themselves, "I know I'm feeling something. What is it?" It can take some time before the answers are prompt and correct. It's something you need to work on with the support and advice of counselors or your twelve-step group. This is a rule that applies to all aspects of recovery, not just sex.

There are a great many misconceptions and false notions about chemical dependence, sex, and recovery. One of the most common is the so-called rule that you shouldn't reenter a sexual relationship until you have been abstinent for a year. A widely repeated remark is made by recovering alcoholic Lewis Meyer in his book *Off the Sauce*: "No alcoholic can know the whole wonder, excitement, and completeness of the sex act until he has been off the sauce *for at least a year!*"

It may be true or it may not, and it may be true for some people but not others. To state it categorically is even more unrealistic than a doctor telling you that you won't be able to play tennis again after your shoulder surgery for exactly six months. He might with justification say to you that the average recovery time is six months, or that he recommends that you don't try it until after six months without checking with him first, or even that three to six months or six to nine months is the usual recovery period. And he might also add that since your surgery was not as difficult as some, you might recover in three weeks—or since it was more extensive and complicated than usual, you should wait at least seven months.

There is no magic number about any aspect of recovery. People who are very experienced in twelve-step groups recommend that newly recovering dependents shouldn't rush through the steps: some say you shouldn't work on the harder steps, such as making a list of your character defects, for at least six months; some say you should take at least a year to work through all twelve steps. But these are not magic numbers either and nobody would insist on them. You shouldn't rush into any part of recovery, including sex, without doing the necessary groundwork. But no one should give you a strict timetable for the redevelopment of intimacy and the resumption of sexual activity. "It happens when it happens" is a much better guideline.

Complicating Factors

Among the sexual problems that sometimes complicate recovery are homosexuality, sexual addiction, and sexual or physical abuse and incest.

Everything that has been discussed here about sexual partnerships and recovery applies almost equally to heterosexual and homosexual relationships. But the additional problem faced by some gay men and lesbians is secrecy and silence. It is essential that homosexuals find a way to be open and honest about their sexual preferences when talking to their counselors and their twelve-step sponsors. These people will accord you the respect and the right to express your feelings that is due to anyone in any kind of nonexploitive sexual partnership. Any recovering chemical dependent who detects any hesitance or bias about sexual preferences from a counselor or sponsor should promptly seek a replacement.

Sexual addiction is being revealed as a more widespread problem than may have been thought, and many people may be covering up the pain of sexual addiction by drinking or taking drugs. Unresolved compulsive sexual behavior will make it almost impossible to recover from chemical addiction; people who have this problem should seek out a Sex Addicts Anonymous program.

Sexual abuse and incest are among the most severe of all sexual problems among chemical dependents and children of alcoholics; the incidence of victims among people in dependence-treatment centers is often staggeringly high. Chemical dependence is found in as many as half of all families in which incest has occurred, and as many as eighty-five percent of female clients of halfway houses have been found to be incest victims.

What complicates the problem even more is that many incest victims avoid twelve-step programs because they don't believe they can speak about their experience, and fearing intimacy they avoid mutual-help groups. Some are so afraid of being touched that they stay away from programs where it is widely known that hugging is a popular practice.

If it is true that children of alcoholics or addicts suffer shame, then the child who additionally has suffered sexual abuse—particularly incest—lives with an even greater burden of shame. Victims of sexual or physical abuse inevitably come to believe that it was their fault, that somehow they caused it either by being a "bad child" who deserved the abuse as punishment, or by being seductive (however unconsciously). As adults such people seem unable to stop apologizing for themselves, justifying themselves, behaving in ways that seem to be constantly asking others to forgive them even for being alive. They may tend to become "people pleasers" who quickly shoulder the blame for everything that goes wrong and automatically sacrifice their own needs for the needs of others. At the same time, such people are torn by conflicting emotions, chiefly anger. To the objective observer, this anger is obviously justifiable, but for victims it is accompanied by the contradictory feeling that they have no right to be angry since the whole thing was their fault in the first place. These contradictory feelings can be severely crippling to the adult child of an alcoholic or addict and almost paralyzing to the victim who in turn becomes an alcoholic or addict—a common aftermath. Certainly all such people are totally lacking in trust, which makes it even more difficult for them to submit to the process of recovery through twelve-step programs; these require a trusting surrender of the ego and will to the guidance of the group and the sponsor. Yet it is the need to be able to trust again that is vital to the recovery of such victims.

Thus, while professional counseling is essential for incest victims, twelve-step programs offer an avenue to recovery that provides factors not even professional help can offer. Incest victims who are chemically dependent commonly testify that when they finally were able to speak of their experience in a twelve-step women's group, and found that their admission was met with the same acceptance and support given to the life histories of other chemical dependents, they felt free of guilt and shame and isolation for the first time in their lives.

It is the essence of the power of such groups that they consist of people who have all felt guilt, shame, and pain, who have compassion and concern for all others who have felt the same things, and that they make no moral judgments of anyone. For the incest victim as for anyone else with sexual difficulties or hang-ups, this is the one most indispensable aid to recovery.

What If Your Spouse Is Still Drinking?

There is one intimacy problem that nothing you have learned yet will allow you to handle wisely or even safely, and that is living with a spouse or partner who is still actively dependent on alcohol or drugs. It is not possible for a recovering alcoholic or addict—or anyone else, for that matter—to have a normal relationship with an active chemically dependent partner.

The active partner will resent you because your recovery threatens his or her own continued drinking or drug use. The partner will resort to almost anything to undermine recovery, from pleas and appeals to scorn. You will also find it difficult if not impossible to refrain from trying to lure or drag your partner into recovery with you. You will want to "sell" your twelve-step program, or hold yourself up as an example, or try to demonstrate dramatically how much better recovery is. You will never succeed in getting your partner to change unless the partner is ready and self-motivated. Meanwhile, you will be using up energy you need for your own recovery; you will be distracted from the work you need to do to make progress, and you will be frustrated and defeated by your inability to change your partner. Living with a chemically dependent spouse while you're trying to recover is like running on the proverbial treadmill; you're not going anywhere, and you'll probably wear yourself out trying.

Your wisest choice is to separate at least temporarily from your partner. A separation may provide the motivation for your partner to seek help, with the realization that the relationship may be permanently jeopardized by continuing chemical dependence. More importantly, a temporary separation will relieve you of the emotional turmoil of the relationship and allow you to concentrate on your recovery. It will also give you a chance to reflect on whether you really want to resume the relationship. You may discover, as many do, that the gifts of recovery are too precious to risk by going back, or that the relationship was not really as good as you had deceived yourself into believing while you were chemically dependent. As one of my female patients said, "Our life together had been one long uninterrupted party; when I stopped drinking and drugging, I realized that there wasn't anything to the relationship except that."

A recovery person is often surprised by the many aspects of their lives that will be touched by recovery. Recently one of my recovering patients remarked, "You know, I'm a married man with two kids, but I realize now that I knew nothing about sex. From my college days on, it was always, 'let's get drunk and get laid.' Sex and alcohol, alcohol and sex. A few years ago, it became alcohol and alcohol, with no sex at all. But now, I've been sober for six months, and it's almost as if I'm a virgin again. I mean I'm doing what I used to do, but I'm *feeling* so much more.'' This rejuvenation is what recovery is all about. I tell my patients to expect a sensory explosion. The addict knows how drugs can take over all the senses, but only the recovering addict knows what it's like to reexperience these long dormant senses.

8

OUTSIDE REHAB: FINDING
YOUR PLACE IN THE WORLD

NOW YOU ARE CLEAN AND SOBER. WHAT HAPPENS NEXT?

As you reenter the world after leaving rehabilitation or joining a twelve-step group, you will find yourself in a crucial and difficult place. You have not arrived anywhere; you have just started out. You are in transition.

If you have not been in treatment but have begun recovery by joining a twelve-step group, you may be confused and perhaps intimidated by the discovery that you are expected to do a lot of things you didn't anticipate. For example, you don't just go to meetings, you are asked to make coffee and clean up afterward, to come early and stay afterward to talk to other members, to find a sponsor and start working on the steps. You are not yet experienced enough to feel comfortable with some of these activities, and you are not clear why they are important or even necessary.

If you have been in treatment, you are leaving a place where you were sheltered, understood, and felt loved. And you're going back out without knowing what kind of reception you're going to get.

How will you fit in? Will your family forgive you? Will your friends still welcome you? Should you go back to work right away, or take some time off? If you don't have a job, will you be able to land one? What about the unpaid bills, the messy apartment, the dozens of details you've been neglecting?

Will life really be any better than when you were drinking or taking drugs?

The answer to all of these questions, especially the last, depends on another question: Are you willing to work for it?

You may have thought that all you have to do is just stay away from your favorite chemical, but fairly early in recovery you should begin to realize that there's much more to it than that. This early period is a time of learning—that recovery involves changing your beliefs, attitudes, and behavior, and that alcoholics and drug addicts *can* do these things. This is the time for keeping always in your mind the principle that the goal of recovery is abstinence from all mood-altering chemicals *and improvement of the way you live your life*. Without the second part of that principle, the first will be difficult if not impossible.

You're certain to encounter hurdles: influences, attitudes, and opinions—whether conscious or unconscious, well-meaning or malicious—that could impede your recovery. That's what we'll be dealing with in this chapter: sizing up these hurdles and then mentally jumping them, one at a time. Keep in mind that *you* have accepted responsibility for your own recovery, and you must be allowed to get on with it. You'll accomplish this with the wise guidance of your rehab therapists, your aftercare counselors, your twelve-step sponsor, and your recovering friends. You are not to be tricked, maneuvered, blackmailed or seduced into thoughts and actions that will destroy this second (and possibly last) chance to live a good life.

Remember: Don't Make Big
Decisions Right Away

This is not the time to sell or buy a house, get a divorce, or fall in love. Of course, some changes may have to be made. If you've never had a job, it's a good time to get one, but if you already have a job, don't change jobs unless you must (for example, if your old job exposes you to a lot of drinking, or if your boss or co-workers aren't giving you support in your recovery). Any big decision that can be avoided or postponed should be.

Why? Aren't you clean and straight? Can't you handle your life now that you're not handcuffed by your chemical? Now that you are going home from rehab or have successfully survived those critical first ninety days of abstinence, aren't you in the clear, over the hump, ready to take on anything? Shouldn't you wipe the whole slate clean and start all over?

If recovery were nothing more than abstinence, the answer would certainly be yes. But it isn't. You are not yet the person you are going to become. During rehab, hospitalization, or the minimum period of counseling or twelve-step participation, you have been to a great extent sheltered and inwardly focused. Especially if you were in a resident treatment program, you were isolated from the temptations and hassles and distractions of "out there." You have probably been so concentrated on the immediate effort—staying clean for a certain period of time—that your mind was relatively free of other concerns.

Some people are frightened by the prospect of leaving rehabilitation or intense counseling; others are impatient to be out on their own and full of confidence that they can handle whatever comes their way.

In either case, all you have really done so far is close the door on chemical dependence and knock at the door of recovery. You have a lot more to learn and accept. This is not a negative thought; the process holds the promise of a completely new and happier kind of life. But first you have to get rid of the old one, and it doesn't just go into the trash with the last bottle or last stash of drugs. It takes a basement-to-attic housecleaning of your thinking, habits, and behavior.

Remember: Play It Safe at Work

A big issue is whether to talk at work about your rehab and recovery. That depends.

If you're applying for a new job, your choices are fairly simple. If you are asked directly whether you have a history of alcoholism or drug use, the only wise decision is to tell the truth. If you lie and get caught later, it will be worse for you. A company that isn't able to accept your situation, and deal with it reasonably and helpfully, probably isn't a good place for you to work anyway.

If you're not asked any direct questions, however, don't volunteer the information.

If you're returning to your old job, the company and at least some of your co-workers probably know about your situation already. If the company has an employee assistance program (EAP) that has helped pay for your rehabilitation and offers some ongoing support, you're in a very good place. Companies that offer EAPs realize that it is far better, from a moral and economic perspective, to help a worker get treatment rather than either retraining a new employee, or suffering through the decreased productivity and increased safety risk posed by a substance-abusing employee.

REMEMBER:
You May Be Asked for Names

One thing you will not have to worry about too much on your job: dealing directly with fellow employees who are still drinking or taking drugs. Now that you're committed to sobriety, you're the last person they want to see. They will stay as far away from you as they can.

But if you reached treatment through an employee assistance program, your employer may eventually ask you if you know of other employees who are still drinking or using. This raises some delicate issues:

- **You have a right not to answer this question.** Even if you're grateful to your company for steering you toward help, you are not obligated to provide names. You are responsible for your own recovery, you cannot orchestrate anyone else's recovery. Also, any company that pressures you to inform on your fellow employees may not be truly interested in helping that employee. Just say you don't know.

- **How far will you be sticking your neck out?** Employee assistance programs are generally very confidential, but companies may differ. Before you mention any co-worker's name, find out if your identity will be kept confidential and what the likely outcome from your actions will be. Will the co-worker be offered treatment, fired, or simply warned?

- **Giving a name may help someone.** On the other hand, if you know of another employee who has a problem with drinking or drugs, your company's confidential employee assistance program may be able to help him as much as it helped you.

- **Giving a name might save an innocent life.** If you know of someone whose drinking or drug taking on the job endangers other people (a drunken bus driver, for example, or a stoned aircraft mechanic), it's your civic duty to provide that name. Do so right away.

- **Avoid exaggerating.** If your knowledge of someone else's alcohol or drug problem is based only or mostly on hearsay, admit it. You're not being asked to play detective or provide proof.

- **Don't expect to "save" anyone.** Even with the best of intentions, you can't help anybody who doesn't want to be helped. Your primary concern must be your *own* recovery. In any case, the *most* you can do is to alert the employee assistance program if you know someone else in your company has a problem with drinking or drug use. Usually, your employer can't confront that person until his job performance begins to suffer.

REMEMBER:
Your Mental Powers Are Still Returning

In the long run, sobriety does wonders for your ability to keep working at a task without distraction. So if you're back on the job after spending a number of weeks in a rehab program, your first reaction may be surprise and delight that you're getting so much accomplished. Doing your work without alcohol or drugs suddenly seems so simple and obvious.

But what if it's not like that? What if you notice your concentration isn't what it should be? You're not apt to be so busy that your work distracts you at every moment from thoughts of drinking. Maybe you'll think back to when coffee break was time for a line of cocaine or a joint in the rest room. Maybe you'll notice your thoughts wandering back to the days you spent in rehab, or to the AA meeting you attended last night. Maybe you'll daydream your way right through a phone conversation with a client, and then wonder later what it was about.

If you're troubled by distraction or memory lapses, go easy on yourself. For many people in recovery, these are common reactions during the "reentry" period. They do not mean that you're losing your mind! They *do* mean that drinking and/or drugs have taken a toll on your nervous system, and that you're still healing. You can expect these symptoms to abate gradually during your first year of sobriety.

What can you do to help bring back your full mental functioning as quickly as possible?

I described in Chapter Four how *nutrition* can help rebalance your body's supplies of the neurotransmitters dopamine, norepinephrine, and serotonin. Be sure you're actually getting that high-protein breakfast—or, if big breakfasts aren't your thing, a light but protein-rich breakfast followed by a midmorning snack of fruit or yogurt. See to it that you're acquiring the habit of eating regular meals every day. Three meals are a minimum; six mini-meals, rich in protein and vitamins, are even better.

We also spoke about the benefits of regular *exercise* on your physical and mental well-being. For longtime couch potatoes, getting the exercise habit requires effort and devotion. Knowing that vigorous exercise oxygenates and stimulates your brain may be just the stimulus you need to get you up and running (swimming, rowing, jumping rope, or whatever you choose).

You can also help your mind work better by *reducing stress* in your life wherever possible, eliminating emotional distractions that use up your mental energy. Here are three simple, easy ways to cut down on unnecessary stress:

- Get enough sleep. If you're chronically short on sleep, and your job requires you to get up early in the morning, try going to bed early a few times a week—even if you think you "can't get to sleep before midnight." You may surprise yourself. That extra hour or two of sleep could make a lot of difference in the way you feel.

• Streamline your job. When you can, delegate work to others rather than doing every little thing yourself. If you're a mother, insist that your children do certain regular chores as soon as they're old enough. Communicate freely so other people know what you're thinking and what you expect from them.

• Keep within your budget. Buy the car you can afford, not the impressive one that will leave you without money for food or rent.

Finally, with your counselor and your new, recovering friends you can *talk out your concerns* about concentration, memory, and mental function. They'll understand, they'll have tips to offer—and just by listening, they'll make your burden seem lighter.

REMEMBER:
Take New Approaches to Old Problems

One of the pieces of clutter you bring with you into recovery is years or even a lifetime of poor problem solving.

Look at the diagram opposite; it's called the nine-dot problem. The aim is to connect all the dots with four straight lines, never taking the pencil from the paper, so the four lines are connected and continuous. Think about the problem, try to visualize it, and experiment a few times before you give up. Very few people solve it without help.

Now look at the solution at the end of this chapter.

There is a reason why this really simple problem is so difficult. People try to solve it on the basis of an assumption: that the lines can't go outside the square formed by the dots. This probably reflects something about the way we are all taught to do geometric or spatial problems in our early school years. You may have tried a dozen different ways of solving the problem, but all of them were encased in this habitual, "standard" way of problem solving.

In recovery, it is *only* by discarding the old assumptions and looking at problems in a totally different light that a healthy life can begin.

Chemically dependent people are likely to have a difficult time staying clean if they persist in their old "standard" behaviors that so damaged their personal relationships. As the AA saying goes: "If you keep doing what you were doing before, you'll keep getting what you got before."

If you always reacted to interpersonal conflict with anger and shouting you aren't going to resolve any conflicts now by doing the same thing. If you continue to avoid problems by ignoring them, they aren't going to vanish now any faster than they did before.

It has been said that as much as ninety-eight percent of what we do is the result of habit, not choice. Habits are automatic;

choice involves thinking. One of the benefits of rehabilitation programs, aftercare, and twelve-step groups is that they help you learn to think about what you are doing, recognize habitual behavior, learn to change it, and begin to live more by choice than by repeating the same old behaviors. This is one of the reasons for not making any big decisions yet: the danger is that you will make such decisions on the basis of your old ways of thinking before you've had a chance really to learn and apply the new ones. The other reason is that you need all your energy right now for working on recovery—not for making decisions and starting something new while handicapped by your old ideas and attitudes.

REMEMBER:
Tune Out the ''Noise''

One fundamental problem-solving difficulty common to alcoholics and drug abusers is the inability to simplify situations and concentrate on the central issue. Many alcoholics and addicts say they took chemicals to escape at least temporarily from the "noise in my head." The noise came from the habit of thinking you could read other people's minds and anticipating (usually wrongly) what would happen if you did this and then he did that and then she did the other thing. It came from overcomplicating things until they ran around in circles in your head, all the unnecessary, irrelevant, invented details chasing each other around like mad monkeys. (As one alcoholic put it, "I suffered from a terminal disease called 'figuring it out.' ") For example:

You are not happy with your boyfriend, girlfriend, husband, wife, etc. You know it's not working and you ought to break it off. This is clear and simple, and all your instincts tell you so. But here comes the noise:

I'll be so lonely. What will I do on Friday and Saturday nights?

People will think he dropped me. Mary will never speak to me; she fixed us up with our first date.

What will Mom and Dad say? They're hoping I'll marry him. They'll be so disappointed.

How will he manage? He'll be so hurt. He'll just go out drinking with the guys all the time. Or he'll find some girl who won't be as good for him.

He might kill himself. How can I do this to him?

These are all the *wrong* questions. What difference does it make what Mary thinks? Is the unlikely possibility that she might be slightly offended worth ruining your whole future for? And what makes you think she cares? What difference does it make what your parents expect? *They're* not going to marry him. What makes you think you'll be so lonely? Don't you have other friends to be with? You got one boyfriend, won't you get another? What makes you think you are so perfect and irreplaceable that he won't find another person who suits him better?

The only questions you need to ask are these: Are you happy together—not constantly, but *on balance*, or are the quarrels and hassles and anger overwhelming the pleasure you used to take in each other? Do you bring out the best in each other? Is this relationship *good* for you—and especially, for your recovery?

Or perhaps you are tired of your job; it doesn't inspire you very much and you haven't been putting your best effort into it. There are hints that your boss is dissatisfied with your recent performance; you may be fired. You know you should look for another more interesting job, and quickly, while you're still in a good bargaining position from your present job. Here comes the noise:

I haven't been here very long; a new company will think I'm a job-hopper. Maybe the boss won't fire me; so maybe I don't need to quit. It wouldn't be fair to the company after they've spent this much time training me. What will my wife think? She'll say I'm unreliable and irresponsible. I'm settled here; I don't think I can handle anything bigger.

The only question that matters is whether you are happy in this job or probably would be happier in another one—or whether changing jobs will encourage or hinder your recovery. What your boss thinks isn't crucial. He wouldn't hesitate to dismiss *you* if *he* were dissatisfied. You can't guess what your wife will say; she might have been thinking all along that your job has made you unhappy and grouchy. You can talk it over with her and find out what she thinks about whether a job change will be good for you—but not whether it will be good for *her*. Unless it means you are going to starve or be transferred to Antarctica or if your job change will in any way directly injure her, your job decision must be *your* decision, not hers.

Then there is the "noise" that comes from replaying over and over again that scene (with your boss, girlfriend, husband, mother, etc.) in which you came out feeling like the loser. You rewind and fast-forward, changing the dialogue every time, saying the smart things you thought of when it was too late, rewriting not only your part but the other person's, never quite satisfied with the way it plays. Or you anticipate a scene you are about to have, planning in advance exactly what the other person is going to say and how you are going to respond, as if you could control the scene like a movie director.

It isn't possible to revise what has already happened. You can think about it, try to understand what was going on, try to understand why the other person behaved as he did so that next time you can handle it better. You can come to the conclusion that it went wrong because you were (a) ill-prepared, (b) too emotional, (c) too short-tempered, or (d) wrong in the first place, or because the other person had a problem that prevented him from dealing fairly, or all sorts of other reasons. This is a learning and problem-solving process. It is by no means the same thing as rewriting it in your head, scratching away at it like a mosquito bite, making yourself more frustrated and irritable and angry because you can't go back and make it work out your way.

There's nothing wrong with planning for difficult confron-

tations or negotiations. You need to be prepared with facts, or
with a clear idea of what point of view or idea or request you
want to present, or what you want to achieve. But it's senseless
to try to crystal-ball exactly what the other person is going to
say and do, and to write her lines in advance. It never comes
out the way you think it's going to, and all you've done is waste
a lot of brainpower and nervous energy that you need for more
essential things.

REMEMBER:
Keep Problem Solving Simple

Good problem solving involves simplifying the issue until you
can identify what the really crucial point is, and then doing
what's necessary to achieve that point. It also involves letting
go of what's past and done with and can't be changed. Bad
problem solving means obscuring the real issue with egotistical
worries and invented fears, burying your own needs in real or
imagined concerns about what others will think or how they
will be affected, and anticipating and building up mountains of
problems that you *imagine* are going to happen tomorrow or
next week.

Bad problem solving also involves poor handling of personal
relationships, especially touchy situations and potential quarrels.
One of the most common barriers to recovery is the difficulty
that chemically dependent people have in accepting responsibility. They always tend to evade commitments and to shift the
blame for everything onto someone else. A favorite ploy is to
answer a complaint or criticism with a counter-complaint, preferably in a completely irrelevant area. Here's some dialogue that
may sound familiar:

THEM: "I asked you to turn on the answering machine before
you went out. I missed an important call."

YOU: "Well, you forgot to leave the key under the mat for me last night."

Or:

THEM: "Don't hang up on me when you get annoyed. You know I hate it."

YOU: "Well, you walk out of the room when we're in the middle of a fight."

THEM: "You wrote three checks without filling in the stubs in the checkbook. How was I supposed to know there wasn't enough money left in the account to cover the rent check?"

YOU: "How can I make ends meet if you never get a raise?"

None of these answers, obviously, are really responsive; they don't excuse you, they don't address the other person's irritation or unhappiness, and they certainly don't open any dialogue that will lead to a resolution of the problem. The most straightforward answer to all of them is a simple: "I'll try not to do it again." In some cases you can even reply: "I did it because I was very angry with you," or "I was hurt; I wanted to get back at you." These are honest responses that describe how *you* feel in the situation without throwing blame in the other person's face.

REMEMBER:
Accept Responsibility

Then there's another good old standby for avoiding responsibility and shifting the blame: the apology with a "but."

"I'm sorry I yelled and grabbed the phone out of your hand, *but* you were just gossiping and you knew I was in a hurry." "I'm sorry I called you a name, *but* you've called me worse things." "I'm sorry I broke your vase, *but* you shouldn't have put it on that shelf."

In fact, two of the most effective expressions in the human vocabulary are, "I'm sorry" (followed by a period—no "but" or excuse or counter-attack or qualification) and "You're right" (followed by a period). What if you are convinced you were right? Does it matter? Is it an issue in which you'd rather prove you are right or rather stay friends? If you feel you must establish who's right or wrong so that you don't keep replaying the same scene, can you do it by simply stating the facts of the case, describing unemotionally what you think happened, and letting the other person come to a conclusion?

REMEMBER:
Watch for Hidden Attempts at Control

Sometimes your efforts to avoid responsibility are disguised as graciousness and politeness. Examples of these run along the lines of "Whatever you want to do is fine with me," or "I don't care, where do you want to eat?" or "Where do you want to go on vacation?" By appearing to be agreeable and deferential to the other person's needs, you avoid making a statement about your own needs and thereby escape responsibility if things don't work out well: the restaurant is no good, the TV show is a bore, the hotel has no pool, and so on.

Most of these things represent disguised efforts at control, one of the biggest and most troublesome of all problem-solving issues for chemical dependents. You control a situation by putting another person under obligation to you, by preventing them from making an effective complaint or negotiating an issue, by forcing them to accommodate to your behavior; or, in another way, to try to figure out what you really want when you refuse to express any preference, by leaving it up to them to make decisions for both of you and then have to face your resentment or disappointment when their choice isn't at all what you really wanted.

Efforts to exert control can be subtle or direct. You may just walk in when everybody has already started doing a job and

begin directing traffic: "No, Sam, you go get the ladder and let
Mary stir the paint. I'll do the trim on the windows; Ed can
scrape the walls. I don't think that bucket is big enough; there's
a better one in the garage." Or you may make sure that your
project is the one selected by handing it in to your boss a day
early—when your competing associate is out sick. Or just when
your associate is about to make a proposal in a staff meeting,
you bring up the subject of a suggestion he made at the last
meeting—and which you know he hasn't had time to finish and
can't report on yet. You can control people in very simple ways:
you and your friends have agreed to meet at a certain time to
see a particular movie and you show up just too late to catch
that movie—but still in time to go to the one down the street,
which was the one you wanted to see in the first place. These
small manipulations are a sure sign that you are trying to control
people's lives in more serious and complex ways as well.

In recovery, if you are a controlling person, you may find
yourself attempting to use your sobriety as a form of control:
to give off faint or not-so-well-disguised signals that if the other
person continues what they're doing, it may threaten your sobriety. If I have to work late on this project, you might imply,
I might have to use cocaine to keep working. You may find
yourself hinting that if your boss hadn't done so and so, you
wouldn't have had to resort to chemicals in the first place. Watch
out for these attempts at control and realize that they really are
subtle excuses for relapse.

REMEMBER:
Not Everyone Understands Your New Perspective

"Co-ing," enabling, and sabotage occur in hidden forms. Sab-
oteurs may try to "test" your recovery by insisting that alcohol
must be on hand in the house "in case somebody drops over."
They may act sullen and resentful if you are determined to go

to your regular twelve-step meeting when they want to go to a movie. A partner or family member may blurt out that you are in AA to someone you were not ready to confide in; they may overwhelm your simple "No thank you" to the offer of a drink with an excess of explanations and apologies, like "Oh, he mustn't have any. The doctor said it disagrees with him. But he's taking some new medicine now and I'm sure he'll be able to have some another time." Your commitment to aftercare sessions or twelve-step meetings may be attacked or weakened by constant questions like "Do you *have* to go every night?" or "How long do you have to go on attending these things?" or "Couldn't you skip it just this once?"

These are all efforts to control your attitudes and behavior, made so much harder to handle because in treatment or in your group, everyone understood about your dependence and has accepted the fact that it was not due to a character defect but to a susceptibility over which you had no control. "Outsiders" are often ignorant about the nature of chemical dependence and persist in thinking that all your problems would be solved if you just had a little more willpower. Old friends may scoff at the notion that you must remain totally abstinent. "Go ahead, just have one," is a refrain you will unfortunately hear over and over again.

Sometimes it may feel as if all the world is conspiring to make you "have just one." You may not have noticed it before, but you will now: not only in television advertisements but in programs themselves, you are constantly being confronted with people enjoying themselves with cigarettes and alcohol. "Recreational" drug use is referred to far more often than most people realize. Magazine advertisements constantly suggest how pleasant and sexy it is to drink and smoke. If you have been a cocaine user, you are particularly susceptible to "craving cues" from any reference to coke, however negative the message—and you'll be astonished how many references to coke there are in the most popular movies and videotapes.

The first thing that greets you when you sit down at a restaurant is the waiter taking before-dinner drink orders; the second thing is the waiter with the wine list. It will seem at times that there is no escape and nothing to be done except give in. At moments you will begin to wonder if the whole world is right and that you can't fight them all alone. At moments you will also be overwhelmed by self-pity or anger that fate or bad luck has made *you* the "only one" who can't enjoy all these "pleasures."

And while the whole world is giving its approval to "social drinking," even smiling with amused tolerance over the comic drunk or the guys at the bar who are having a little too much, you will discover that the world often takes a different attitude toward those who admit they "can't handle it." While the whole world doesn't seem to think twice about the occasional pot-smoker, the world doesn't seem to have much patience with someone who says he has been in rehabilitation for a cocaine habit.

You will find many understanding and tolerant people; many who have been enlightened by the disease concept of addiction and who accept that you never asked for this problem. You will even find nonalcoholics or nonaddicts who will actually admire you for doing something about it. But unfortunately you will find too many others who consider alcoholism and addiction a symptom of a character disorder, or proof of a weakness of will.

What's wrong with you that you don't have the strength or the sense to drink moderately like other people? How come everybody else drinks without letting themselves progress to having "a disease?" What do you mean "you couldn't help it?"

Not many people will confront you directly with such challenges or with outright accusations. Most people's disapproval will be subtle or fairly well concealed. It may come in the form of a host's or hostess's self-consciousness about offering you a drink—or not offering you one, and then perhaps watching surreptitiously to see if you do "sneak" something alcoholic. Because you need to avoid the "people, places, and things" that might arouse cravings or tempt you to drink or take drugs, you should have dropped out of your regular poker game or your regular cocktails-first lunch with women friends. If you haven't, you may suddenly find yourself not being invited—either because your friends don't feel comfortable drinking or taking drugs when you don't, or because they're afraid you will feel uncomfortable. Their behavior may not stem from concern about your recovery, but from their own fear of embarrassment. People may shy away from you because they assume you will disapprove of their drinking or taking drugs, however much you may have communicated to them that you don't judge what they do, you just know you don't dare do it yourself.

When you have only recently changed your drinking and drugging habits, these situations will be very uncomfortable, and you may find yourself resenting people's lack of understanding or acceptance. There is very little to do about it except to be understanding and tolerant yourself. Nobody except another alcoholic or addict can really *know* how you feel or think, and people's prejudices, ignorance, and selfish fears are something everybody has to live with at some time in their lives. After you have been in recovery for a while, you will feel such confidence in the rightness and benefits of what you are doing that other people's attitudes will be insignificant.

REMEMBER:
If Other People Have a Problem with Your Program, It's *Their* Problem.

One of their problems may stem from the fact that you yourself and the people you know probably have certain expectations about your recovery that may be quite unrealistic. You may have thought it would be quick, simple, and easy, and that the hardest part would be getting through that first day without a drink or a drug. It doesn't take most people very long to find

out that, yes, the first day was hard, the second day not quite
so bad, and succeeding days easier and easier, but then the work
of remaking yourself begins, and that's not a breeze. They may
have thought that once you stopped drinking and drugging,
and especially once you got out of rehab or got yourself into
some kind of treatment or support program, you would be so
completely transformed that life together would hold no more
problems.

What they have to learn is now that you are back to "normal,"
you will display all of the "normal" person's susceptibility to
life's stresses, to have ups and downs, good and bad moods,
moments of anger and temper. An effective treatment program
will help you to become a better person and to deal more effectively with anger, resentment, and mood swings. But not
even the most successful recovery program has ever claimed to
make people perfect. While you are working toward achieving
the "new you," those around you will eventually begin to recognize that not only are you *trying* to change, you *are* changing.
They may even begin to change with you. Meanwhile, you
will find it easier to accept their adjustment difficulties by relying
on your own new problem-solving approaches and attitudes.

REMEMBER:
Cultivate a Healthy Selfishness

If you are a parent (particularly a mother), you may have spent
a lot of time and emotional energy "living inside" your children—meaning feeling their feelings, suffering their pain, worrying out their decisions. Mothers in particular are so empathic
with their children that they almost automatically hurt when
their child is hurt. One mother whose daughter was having
emotional problems over her weight said to the family therapist,
"When my daughter gets up in the morning and gets on the
scales, if she comes out of the bathroom frowning I know I'm

going to have a bad day." The therapist responded, "No, it means *she's* going to have a bad day." This is a distinction chemically dependent parents must learn to make, to withdraw and separate their feelings—not their concern or their interest or their sympathy, but their *feelings*—from their children's. If you are so closely enmeshed with your child that you can't be even the least bit objective, you are going to be crippled in your efforts to help that child solve problems or to solve your own.

An important lesson you need to learn is the difference between healthy selfishness and egotistical selfishness. It is necessary for recovery that you be selfish in the sense that you ask yourself first and foremost what will be best for your recovery, and that you concern yourself about others only if your decisions or actions will hurt them. Chemically dependent people have a lot of work to do toward rebuilding their lives and rediscovering who they are; they have to simplify their thoughts and actions and stop trying to involve others and control others. If you run yourself crazy worrying about every single possible ramification of your actions, many of which won't happen anyway and most of which you can't control in the first place, you will very quickly find yourself seeking relief from your old "friend" the chemical. You have to learn to mind your own business and take care of your own business and to realize that the whole world does not revolve around you. This is part of the work of recovery. It turns out to be far less selfish than it may seem when you realize that if you take care of your own needs in recovery, everybody close to you will be better off.

REMEMBER:
"Outside" Problems Don't Disappear

At the very beginning of their "reentry" into the world, most recovering alcoholics and addicts feel a great upsurge of enthusiasm and confidence. This feeling, which can last a month or more, gives way temporarily when optimism and energy fade a little. You gradually discover that many of the problems you had before recovery began are still there. The only difference is that now you aren't drinking or taking drugs.

That is, however, the most important difference in the world. Life is difficult for everybody, but it's a lot less difficult for you now that you have a clear mind, a healthier body, and a positive program for your life.

You cannot too often remind yourself, especially during the rocky days of early abstinence, that recovery brings with it far more than the ability to refrain from drinking or taking drugs. It brings with it even more than the ability to do this *comfortably*. At the beginning, you may find it hard to see or to really imagine how different you and your life will be, but you may begin to really incorporate this possibility into your thinking and feeling by concentrating on the example of others, such as the more experienced members of your twelve-step group, or sometimes just from reading the paper.

On the sports page of *The New York Times* of July 20, 1989, is an account of the fall and rise of Lonnie Smith, "the thirty-three-year-old hot-hitting Braves outfielder," who was a star player with the St. Louis Cardinals when he was twenty-seven—and an ex-player with nowhere to go when he was thirty-one.

"I was an addict the very first time I took drugs, never mind all that stuff about it being a gradual thing," Smith is quoted in the *Times*. "I started for the usual reasons; because I was curious, because I thought it was the thing to do, but the big thing was I couldn't stop. And then I literally couldn't get through the day without it."

Smith finally got himself into rehabilitation, but his ball-playing afterward was undistinguished at best, and by 1986 he was without a job. Finally given a chance in the minor leagues, he fought his way back to the top, and in 1989 he was named the National League Comeback Player of the Year.

"For Smith, aside from a tremendous pride in craft and a

desire to keep earning a living, the reasons for his remarkable turnaround probably lie more in what he has gone through off the field than on," wrote *Times* sportswriter David Falkner. "He simply knows more about who he is and where he has been."

Smith said that, even more than playing baseball for another few years, his goal was to establish a secure life on the other side of the nightmare he had lived through.

According to Falkner, he may already have accomplished that goal. Before his drug problems, Lonnie Smith had always wanted to wear a single earring; it seemed beautiful to him, an old African custom that represented the attainment of manhood. But he would never allow himself to wear one. Recently he asked his new fiancée what she thought about a man who wears an earring, and she told him it would be beautiful. He's been wearing an earring ever since.

The solution to the nine-dot problem on page 203:

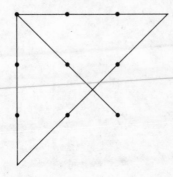

9

LIFETIME STRATEGIES AND
REWARDS

ONE OF THE MOST TREASURED OF ALL THE PASSAGES IN AA LIT-
erature is one that is referred to as "The Promises":

> If we are painstaking about . . . our development, we will
> be amazed before we are half way through. We are going
> to know a new freedom and a new happiness. We will not
> regret the past or want to shut the door on it. We will
> comprehend the word serenity and we will know peace.
> No matter how far down the scale we have gone, we will
> see how our experience can benefit others. That feeling
> of uselessness and self pity will disappear. We will lose
> interest in selfish things and gain interest in our fellows.
> Self-seeking will slip away. Our whole attitude and out-
> look upon life will change. Fear of people and economic
> insecurity will leave us. We will intuitively know how to
> handle situations which used to baffle us . . .

This is a breathtaking inventory of benefits, one that the more
skeptical observer might dismiss as being not only unrealistic

but sentimental. You may find it difficult to believe that you might actually attain a life this good, and even more difficult to believe the testimony of many recovering chemical dependents that in fact they *have* experienced these rewards. If so, then perhaps you might at least file them away somewhere: look at the list again when you are a year or two into recovery. You may be surprised.

What is particularly interesting about this passage is that although it was written in the 1930s, it encompasses almost every issue that modern psychologists recognize as being crucial to successful long-term recovery from chemical dependence.

- The need for a "painstaking" attention to the work of recovery. It is not something about which you can be casual, sloppy, or indifferent.

- The necessity for eliminating unhealthy guilt while recognizing and accepting the damage done by the dependence.

- The healing power of accepting life without railing and screaming about its painfulness or unfairness.

- The community of all people, the commonality of their experience, and the rewards of communicating and relating.

- The detrimental effect on growth of self-pity, selfishness, self-seeking, self-hatred, and fear.

- The distorting of natural instincts and responses that is caused by chemicals and the importance of restoring these to health.

The list could be considered as a rough road map to what long-term recovery is all about and how one travels along that road.

At the beginning of recovery, inpatient or outpatient rehabilitation, and twelve-step group participation can do wonders. They support you through the worst days of early abstinence, and show you how to keep maintaining it. That is an essential and vital start. But if you think it's all you need or all you want, you will fall back into your chemical dependence in practically no time.

The trouble is that the transformations of early recovery are largely based on emotional upheaval. That's good; that's just what is needed at that stage. But these transformations will be short-lived if they are not integrated with more fundamental long-term changes: new ways of feeling, new insights into how you think and behave, new priorities and values. These add up to a whole new way of being—or rather, of becoming, because the work of discovering yourself and learning how to live in this new way is never finished.

Sam, an ex-patient at the Outpatient Recovery Center and a recovering alcoholic, says that after he had been going to AA meetings for a few days he suddenly realized "that these people are serious. They really mean it. They're talking about doing this for the rest of their lives." He was so terrified by the idea that he went off on a three-day binge. But Sam came back, because somehow through the alcoholic haze he also came to realize that if he started drinking again, that too, was for the rest of his life.

Recovery leads to growth and gives you an opportunity to make the rest of your life better and better. The other way leads back to the hell you came from, to an unhappy life and a short one.

But those who think that recovery—even in its largest sense of fundamental personal growth and change—will automatically bring happiness, solve all problems, and forestall all pain are fated for disappointment. Recovery is not a magic wand.

People who have achieved "good sobriety"—solid recovery—who have remained drink- and drug-free for years, can be as profoundly unhappy as anybody else. But that's the point. Real life—sober life—consists of many emotions: joy, hope,

contentment, and also anger, sadness, depression, and sometimes despair. People who are recovering successfully can suffer
from a desire to drink or take drugs and can even relapse—
usually when they have drifted away from their support systems. But in all the ways that matter, they are *infinitely* better
off than when they were active chemical dependents, and in
most cases vastly better off than people *who never had their problem*. If they stay in touch with their support systems they have
the tremendous advantage of an instant source of understanding,
guidance, and reassurance. Most people never have that.

Recovery Lasts a Lifetime

Recovery is a lifetime process. It requires lifetime strategies.

The short-term techniques you learn in early recovery—
overcoming denial, resisting temptation, preventing relapse—
do exactly what they are designed to do, but no more. The
lifetime strategies help you eliminate alcoholic thinking and
poor problem solving, build self-esteem and self-respect, instill
a devotion to honesty, and reveal the pleasure and utility of
sharing.

Many recovering drug users and alcoholics describe themselves as "grateful" for their disease. They would rather *not*
have had the disease in the first place, but having had it, they
are grateful that it has led them to discover a self they never
knew and an opportunity to change and develop. Without the
disease, they feel, they probably would have done what most
people do: just go on the same way, doing the same things,
reacting and responding in the same fashion, not learning or
changing.

It is interesting that in recent years, the medical/psychiatric
community has begun preaching what AA has been practicing
for fifty years: that life-style change is the pathway to recovery.

It *is* possible to recover from alcoholism or drug dependence without such programs. People have done it. But far fewer people succeed on their own compared to those who are active in AA, NA, CA, and related twelve-step programs. Even those who do recover solo have a much harder time of it, and they're missing out on one of the few actual "bonuses" of addiction recovery: the benefit of lifelong support from a whole host of people who understand what they've been through.

Twelve-step groups offer a great deal to the recovering chemical dependent. First, and on the most primitive level, they give you a place to go and something to do during those hours when you used to be drinking or taking drugs—hours that are now empty because you haven't yet built a new life that will give you something to fill them. Meetings keep you away from temptation at the most dangerous hours. Second, if you have been in rehabilitation they offer a substitute "safe house" for at least part of the day, to help you through the transition from total security to being completely on your own. Many recovering people find an effective plan is to work during the day and attend twelve-step meetings in the evening. Third, they are the best place to learn the techniques of keeping clean and of changing your life. They give you something to look forward to. Finally, and most important of all, they are where you will find encouragement, hope, support, and unlimited opportunities for making new friends who understand you, can identify with your problems and pain, care about you, and be there when you need them—which is probably a great deal more than you can say about even the best friend you ever had before.

In an article about alcoholic and drug-addicted medical professionals, Dr. John Sternberg of Baltimore, quotes a recovering thirty-two-year-old physician:

I suppose that just as my addiction to drugs and alcohol persisted out of attempts to feel better, my attendance at AA and NA has persisted because these meetings do indeed make one feel better. Unlike drugs and alcohol, the good feelings produced by AA and NA are genuine. They come from within.

It has been some time since my last use of drugs and alcohol, yet my attending AA/NA meetings is at a greater frequency than it was early on in my addiction.

The fellowship has so much more to offer me than merely stopping my active addiction. AA/NA meetings help me to achieve new levels of personal, emotional and spiritual growth. Early in my addiction, I did not want to recover. I simply wanted to get the Medical Society off my back. With further attendance, I came to be envious of the quality of life I saw exhibited by those members in recovery. Eventually I wanted what they had . . . I have been given the greatest gift of all—the freedom to be myself and to like and respect myself.

These groups provide what all human beings need—and what chemically dependent people need more than anyone: recognition by others of their "humanness," affirmation of their value as human beings, and validation of their feelings.

Actor Tony Curtis was quoted in *Newsweek* as having his own fond vision of the future for recovering chemical dependents: "I see instead of having bars every few blocks, we should have little therapy centers where you can pull your car over and have a chance to talk to somebody."

In fact, that's just what twelve-step groups do. When you're on vacation, or if you're alone in a strange place, your guard may be down. Don't wait for temptation to turn into relapse. Remember that your sponsor is always available for telephone support. Also, you can find an AA meeting (and increasingly, NA and CA meetings) anywhere in the world. So before leaving on your trip, phone AA and find out exactly when and where there is a meeting in destinations as diverse as Paris, Stockholm, Pagopago, Alaska, and Hawaii. Unlike most people, members of twelve-step groups can move into a new town and within hours have the beginnings of dozens of close friendships. Uni-

versity of Michigan psychiatrist Dr. Randolph Nesse calls this
"a friendly, small-town universe, instead of the drug-ridden
combat area millions of Americans inhabit. Maybe people in
these . . . groups are in fact re-creating a more natural and
normal environment for themselves. literally providing something missing from modern life . . . just at the point in society
when both the extended family and the nuclear family are breaking down."

One of the most significant reasons that aftercare and continuing
group participation are so essential is that true lifetime recovery
involves a lot of *practice* of coping skills and repeated reminders
of new ways of thinking and problem solving. Twelve-step
meetings are attended by large numbers of alcoholics and addicts
who have been in recovery for as long as fifteen or twenty
years. They keep attending not only for fellowship and reinforcement but also to refresh their outlook. It's common to hear
one of these "veterans" respond to a newcomer's comments
with "Thanks for reminding me." One reason is that people in
recovery for a long time have incorporated most of the new
"rules for living" so deeply into their behavior that they don't
think about it anymore; but since none of us are perfect, they
forget some of the rules or make mistakes in applying them.
They need "booster shots" from time to time. These people
have learned that people change, situations change, and times
change; remaining active in a group provides you with the
"updates" you need to manage these changes. Finally, continuing to go to meetings ensures that you continue to practice.
   What you learn in rehab or in early group participation is
critical, but it's being done under constant regular guidance.
Aftercare and group participation allow these rules to become
solidly embedded in your life-style. It's a matter of the old
saying, "Give a man a fish and he eats for a day; teach him to
fish and he eats for a lifetime."
   So at the beginning of recovery you are being given the rules

of coping on a daily basis; with aftercare and continued group support you will make this learning your own and incorporate these habits into your instinctive feelings and behavior. As the AA saying goes: "You can't think your way out of this disease. You have to feel your way out."

The life changes that must be made by recovering alcoholics and drug dependents differ a great deal from those that are recommended for other people having troubles in their lives; the ordinary psychological self-help books don't apply. Chemically dependent people are different. It doesn't matter—and nobody knows—whether they are different to begin with, or whether they become different in the course of their active dependence. What works for the chemically dependent might work very well for other people, but the reverse is not always true.

For example, in traditional psychotherapy, people are helped to think more clearly about their problems so they know how to act on them; they learn to understand their feelings and analyze their behavior so they can change it. In recovery from chemical dependence; this approach is turned backward. People are taught how to act so they learn how to think. The AA formula is, "Right acting leads to right thinking." Another way of putting it is, "What we practice we become."

This is not exactly a new idea; the great American psychologist William James first suggested it a century ago, but the idea was so contrary to accepted psychology that it was essentially ignored. James said, among other things, that crying makes us sad. In 1989 a group of psychologists demonstrated James's theory with an experiment in which people were given instructions for making certain facial expressions, without being told what those expressions were or what the purpose of the experiment was. Then they were asked to describe their feelings. When the subjects were given instructions that made them produce something like a smile, a frown, or a look of terror, they reported feeling happy, angry, or frightened.

"The truth is, *if you want to change how you feel, you must change*

*how you act and keep at it long enough until acting in a healthy manner
is as comfortable as acting in a self-defeating manner used to be."*

This does *not* mean pretending to feel a particular feeling. It
does *not* mean faking an emotion. It means doing what people
do who feel that way. At the simplest level, for example, not
drinking or taking drugs will eventually make you *feel* like a
nondrinker or non–drug user. When you are required to sit in
front and always speak up in aftercare or group-meeting discussions, you will eventually feel at ease doing so. An observer
can actually see the dramatic change in a newcomer as he
blushes, sweats, and stammers through his first statement to a
group and then gradually begins to speak more openly and easily
and eventually leads a discussion without hesitation or self-
consciousness.

A recovering alcoholic tells the following story. She had always had problems in relationships because she was a do-
gooder, constantly interfering, butting in, and "just trying to
help." She did it even when she didn't have the foggiest idea
what she was talking about: she would respond to people's
requests for travel directions, for example, even when she
wasn't sure of the route! Her sponsor told her that whenever
she had the urge to interfere, she should try "visualizing." She
should make an effort to actually see herself sitting in the back
seat of a car telling the driver how to drive. Then she should
visualize a soundproof glass partition between her and the
driver. At an AA meeting some time later, this recovering alcoholic was sitting near a woman who had identified herself as
being at her first AA session. Halfway through the meeting,
the newcomer got up and left. The recovering alcoholic almost
followed her out, but didn't. Afterward, she asked her sponsor
why nobody went after the woman. What was the rule about
this: weren't AAs supposed to help alcoholics whenever they
could? Shouldn't somebody have tried to persuade her to stay?
The sponsor said no; if the woman had really been ready for
AA, she would have stayed. If she wasn't ready, nobody could
talk her into it and she would only feel trapped and resentful

and might never come back. Then the sponsor asked, "Why didn't you go after her yourself?" "I don't know," the woman replied. "I didn't figure it out. I just felt I should stay where I was. Now that I've had time to think it over, I realize that since I didn't know the rules, I shouldn't do anything. The funny thing is, it didn't bother me. I didn't feel guilty about not helping."

"Now you're getting it," her sponsor said.

Becoming What You Practice

It works at all levels and in all areas of life. Let's say you are the kind of person who's a martyr or a people-pleaser. Perhaps you're this way because you feel you don't deserve to come first or have your own needs met in preference to someone else's, no matter how much more compelling your needs are. It's fine to *tell* yourself, "Yes, I do deserve to have my needs met. I do feel deserving." But you also have to act. What you can do is this:

The next time somebody says, "May I have the last piece of cake?" you say, "No, that's my piece. I haven't had mine yet." If somebody says, "Mom, can you drive me to Mary's house right away?" you answer, "No, I'm busy. Next time you want a ride, ask me in advance and I'll try to work it into my schedule." If somebody says for the third time in a week, "Tom, will you stay after work until those papers are typed so you can read them over and Sue can get them in the mail?" you say politely but clearly, "No, that's Ed's job." And if they say, "But Ed has a dinner date," then you say, "So have I." This will be extremely difficult for you at first; most people-pleasers and martyrs are terrified at the notion of sticking up for their rights. You may find this especially difficult in the case of the overtime request, because people-pleasers are always certain that if they say no to the boss, however unreasonable his request,

they'll get fired. If they're used to your martyr habits, they may
be surprised at first, but they will soon realize that you are
simply doing what everybody else does naturally—protecting
yourself against exploitation. And if you practice the new behavior consistently, two things will happen. Intellectually, you
will begin to recognize that your reasons for saying, "No" or
asking for something are absolutely legitimate, while your reasons for giving in are pathologically self-sacrificing. Second,
you will begin to feel *comfortable* about taking your stand; you
will actually *feel* as if you deserve what you are asking for or
refusing to do. You will begin to feel self-respect, because you
will finally be treating yourself as decently and generously as
you have always treated others.

Once is not enough. The first time you do it and succeed,
you may be so excited you will think you've licked the problem
for good. Don't believe it. It took you years to establish those
habit patterns. They are so firmly rooted in your behavior as
well as your thinking that they are not going to surrender so
easily or quickly. Doing something a different way just once
doesn't change your fundamental feelings. You must practice
and practice until you behave the new way all the time, because
you are *feeling* the new way all the time. You may occasionally
stumble but, just remember that even the greatest violinist can
hit a wrong note when he's learning a beautiful new concerto.

It is also wise not to think too much. Chemically dependent
people seem to become so confused about their feelings that
they don't know what they're feeling, much less understand it.
Thinking often gets in the way of feeling. So, my advice is stop
thinking and start feeling.

Lifetime recovery involves other contradictions and paradoxes that would be too difficult to deal with alone, and which
aftercare and group work will help you to accept and use.

To take charge, you must surrender. To win, you must lose.

As we saw at the beginning of this book, recovery begins
with a seemingly contradictory notion: you must admit that
you are helpless in the face of your chemical dependence; at the

same time, you must take responsibility for ending it. The point is that only *you* can decide to admit that you are powerless. But that admission allows you to accept the power of the recovery process.

This carries over into your relationships with other people, which of course is the central issue of life. A successful marriage or other love relationship, for example, requires that the partners be intimate and bound up with each other, but still autonomous. It's another paradox: you have to "stay separate" from people in order to become intimate. In order to get any control over your life, you must stop trying to control things, including people, that can't be controlled.

Consider that most cherished pieces of advice from AA, the Serenity Prayer: "God grant me the serenity to accept what I cannot change, the courage to change what I can, and the wisdom to know the difference."

The Serenity Prayer is not just a formula repeated by rote at the beginning or end of AA meetings. It is an attitude that twelve-step participants use routinely and regularly to help them get through daily difficulties. It suggests a guide to good problem solving that goes something like this:

Is this problem something I can do anything about at all, either directly or indirectly? If it isn't, I should stop agonizing over it, letting it run around in my brain, getting frustrated, angry, and resentful over it. If it is something I can change, have I got the guts to do it? If not, I should call my sponsor or counselor or a good friend in the group and ask for their encouragement and support. Do I know whether it is something that can be changed or not? Usually the key to this question is: if you can only change it by trying to control somebody else's feelings or behavior, it probably can't be done.

The fact is, we can't control our emotions. Can you accurately and consistently predict how you will feel next Tuesday? Does telling yourself to be confident always make you feel confident? Does someone yelling at you always make you mad? The answer to these questions is no. The absolute best you can do is to accurately and honestly assess your feelings at that moment, and then decide to act appropriately.

All chemically dependent people have poor self-esteem, whether they had it before they became dependent or developed it as a result. People with poor self-image have a terrible time believing they deserve anything good. They feel they have messed up and deserve whatever rotten fate befalls them. If it doesn't happen naturally, they manufacture it or trigger it. They find ways to sabotage or short-circuit relationships, they court disaster until they capture it, they create crises so that they can fail to weather them.

The basic problem for most people in recovery is not fear of failure, but fear of success. If this sounds like you, the solution is to get out of your own way, so you can enjoy the abundant riches of full recovery. It's not a problem of wanting too much, but of believing that too little is attainable.

More recovery paradoxes:

First you are told that chemically dependent people are egocentric and self-centered. You are instructed to break down your ego, admit to all your worst faults, and learn humility. Then you are told that your worst problem is a lack of self-esteem, and in recovery you are advised to build up a sense of yourself and belief in yourself.

How can you reconcile these two propositions? Accept the definition of "ego" as the image you build of yourself out of fear, self-defense, false pride, and dishonesty. Egotism is a determination to protect your self-image at all costs. Then take the definition of selfhood as acceptance of the person you discover yourself to be when you are free of drugs and alcohol, and can take a good long look at yourself in your recovery mirror. True self-esteem involves an acceptance of that person, imperfections and all. When you can destroy the fake, self-centered ego and discover the core goodness that had been buried underneath, you will have resolved the paradox of recovery.

Listen to a group session and you will hear someone say he used to describe himself as "the most generous guy in the world," or a woman describe herself as "the most unselfish mother who ever lived," and then confess that the generosity was all self-serving ("Sure, I'd be generous to you if it would eventually do me some good") and the unselfishness was egocentric ("I thought everybody would love me if I always gave them what they wanted"). After facing the truth about themselves, these people could then legitimately say, "I'm not much more or less selfish than the next person" or "Yes, I've been selfish, but that's something I can work on."

In the bad old days, your self-worth was something you felt you had to earn, minute by minute, through who you knew and what you achieved. But those days are receding into the past. Increasingly, as your recovery progresses, your self-worth takes root and stands on its own. This is not a one-time act, but a gradual process that develops as you cultivate awareness instead of denial, honesty instead of secrecy, and spiritual openness instead of arrogance. It's not just recovery you're discovering. It's integrity.

NATIONAL RESOURCES FOR
RECOVERY

For more information on Recovery and Substance Abuse, you may wish to contact:

1-800-COCAINE

1-800-HELPLINK
The computer-assisted, toll free, and confidential informational and referral service of Fair Oaks Hospital.

1-800-LIFENET
The Information and Referral Network for Emotional and Substance Abuse Problems in the Greater New York area.

Adult Children of Alcoholics
P.O. Box 35623
Los Angeles, CA 90035

Alanon Family Group (including Alateen)
Box 862
Midtown Station
New York, NY 10018-6106

Alcoholics Anonymous
Box 459
Grand Central Station
New York, NY 10163

Cocaine Anonymous
P.O. Box 1367
Culver City, CA 90232

International Doctors in Alcoholics Anonymous
1950 Volney Road
Youngstown, OH 44511

International Lawyers in Alcoholics Anonymous
Suite 200
111 Pearl Street
Hartford, CT 06103

Marijuana Smokers Anonymous
135 South Cypress
Orange, CA 92666

Narcotics Anonymous
P.O. Box 9999
Van Nuys, CA 91409

National Association for Children of Alcoholics
31706 Coast Highway, Suite 201
South Laguna, CA 92677

National Clearinghouse for Alcohol and Drug Information
5600 Fishers Lane
Rockville, MD 20852
(301) 468-2600

PRIDE
Parents' Resource Institute for Drug Education
50 Hurt Plaza
Suite 210
Atlanta, GA 30303
1-404-577-4500

RECOMMENDED READING

For additional reading material on all aspects of recovery, I suggest that you consult the following books:

Bradshaw, John E. *Bradshaw on the Family: A Revolutionary Way of Self-Discovery.* Deerfield Beach, Fla.: Health Communications, Inc., 1988.

Bradshaw, John E. *Healing the Shame That Binds You.* Deerfield Beach, Fla.: Health Communications, Inc., 1988.

Many of my patients have found these two books by John Bradshaw to be very helpful in understanding how addiction affects the entire family.

Cermak, Timmen L. *Diagnosing and Treating Codependence: A Guide for Professionals Who Work with Chemical Dependents, Their Spouses and Children.* Johnson Institute, 1986.

While Cermak's book is aimed at the professional therapist, a few of my patients—and many individuals on my staff—consider this book helpful.

Each Day a New Beginning. Harper Religious Books, Div. of Harper & Row, San Francisco. 1985.

Touchstones. Harper Religious Books, Div. of Harper & Row, San Francisco. 1987.

These two spiritual books are "meditation books," designed to provide emotional and spiritual support through the difficult times of recovery. *Each Day a New Beginning* is written for female recovering addicts, while *Touchstones* is designed for men.

Gold, Mark S. *The Good News About Depression.* New York: Villard Books, 1987.

Gold, Mark S. *The Good News About Panic, Anxiety, and Phobias.* New York: Villard Books, 1989.

Anxiety and depression are two of the most common conditions associated with addiction and recovery. These books are ideal for the recovering person suffering from either anxiety disorders or clinical depression since they emphasize the biological basis of these disorders while discussing the most effective treatments.

Gravitz, Herbert L., Bowden, Julie D. *Recovery: A Guide for the Adult Children of Alcoholics.* New York: Simon & Schuster, 1987.

A very helpful book that discusses the special problems in recovery for the ACOA.

Larsen, Earnest. *Stage II: Recovery: Life Beyond Addiction.* San Francisco: Harper & Row, 1985.

Larsen, Earnest. *Stage II: Relationships: Love Beyond Addiction.* San Francisco, Perennial Library, 1987.

Living Sober. Alcoholics Anonymous World Services, Inc., 1986. A true classic in the field of recovery.

Madara, Edward J., and Abigail Meese (eds.). *The Self-Help Sourcebook: Finding and Forming Mutual Aid Self-Help Groups* (second edition). Denville, N.J.: Self-Help Clearinghouse, Saint Clares–Riverside Medical Center, 1988.
A thorough listing of national self-help groups on a wide variety of subjects, including divorce, alcoholism, and sexual abuse.

Maxwell, Ruth. *The Booze Battle*. New York: Ballantine Books, 1986.
One of the classics on the subject of alcoholism, its straight-forward approach will be helpful to anyone who has questions about the disease.

Maxwell, Ruth. *Beyond the Booze Battle*. New York: Ballantine Books, 1988.
Explores the codependent role of those who live with alcohol abusers and helps them find guidance and support for themselves.

Robertson, Nan. *Getting Better: Inside AA*. New York: Morrow, 1988.
A fascinating book that describes the most important phenomena in recovery: Alcoholics Anonymous.

Slaby, Andrew. *Aftershock: Surviving the Delayed Effects of Trauma, Crisis, and Loss*. New York: Villard Books. 1989.
For many recovering people, their addiction is intimately connected to a traumatic event or crisis in their lives. Dr. Slaby discusses how these events can ruin our lives, while presenting good, commonsense approaches to treatment.

Wholey, Dennis. *The Courage to Change*. Boston: Houghton Mifflin, 1984.

Intimate and hopeful conversations with "celebrity" recovering addicts. Many of my patients find reading about these success stories to be very helpful.

SOURCES

Asghar, Khursheed: "Role of dietary and environmental factors in drug abuse," in *Alcohol and Drug Research*, Vol. 7 (1986). Pergamon Journals Ltd.

Associated Press. "Outpatient Treatment Helpful For Alcoholics." *The New York Times* (February 14, 1989).

Bissell, LeClair and Jane K. Skorina. "One Hundred Alcoholic Women in Medicine: An Interview Study." *Journal of the American Medical Association* 257:21 (June 5, 1987):2939–2944.

Blum, Kenneth and Michael C. Trachtenberg. "Addicts May Lack Some Neurotransmitters." *The U.S. Journal* (July 1987):16.

Blum, Kenneth and Michael C. Trachtenberg. "Neurochemistry and Alcohol Craving." *California Society for the Treatment of Alcoholism and Other Drug Dependencies News.* 13:2 (September 1986):1–7.

Blum, Kenneth, David Allison, Laurel A. Loeblich, Michael C. Trachtenberg and Richard W. Williams. "Reduction of Both Drug Hunger and Withdrawal Against Advice Rate of Cocaine Abusers in a 30-Day Inpatient Treatment Program by the Neuronutrient Tropamine." *Current Therapeutic Research* 43:6 (June 1988):1204–1214.

Bogdaniak, Ronam C., and Fred P. Piercy. "Therapeutic Issues of

Adolescent Children of Alcoholics (AdCa) Groups." *International Journal of Group Psychotherapy* 37:4 (October 1987):569–588.

Burns, Beatrice R. "Treating Recovering Alcoholics." *Journal of Gerontological Nursing* 14:5 (1988):18–22.

Cain, Arthur H. *The Cured Alcoholic: New Concepts in Alcoholism Treatment and Research* New York: The John Day Company, 1964.

Charles P. O'Brien, and Woody, George E. "Sedative-Hypnotics and Antianxiety Agents." *Annual Review of Psychiatry*, Volume 5 (1986). Washington, D.C.: American Psychiatric Press. 186–187.

Cocores, James A. "Co-Addiction: A Silent Epidemic." *Fair Oaks Hospital Psychiatry Letter* 5:2 (February 1987):5–8.

Cocores, James A. "Outpatient Treatment of Drug and Alcohol Addiction," in *A Handbook of Drug and Alcohol Addiction*, edited by Norman S. Miller. New York: Marcel Dekker, Inc.

Cocores, James A. "Treatment of the Dually Diagnosed Adult Drug User," in *Dual Diagnosis Patients*, edited by Mark S. Gold and Andrew E. Slaby. New York: Marcel Dekker, Inc.

Cocores, James A., Charles A. Dackis and Mark S. Gold. "Sexual Dysfunction Secondary to Cocaine Abuse in Two Patients." *The Journal of Clinical Psychiatry* 47:7 (July 1986):384–385.

Cocores, James A., Mark S. Gold, Mukesh D. Patel, and A. Carter Pottash. "Brief Communication: Cocaine Abuse, Attention Deficit Disorder, and Bipolar Disorder." *The Journal of Nervous and Mental Disease* 175:7 (1987):431–432.

Cocores, James A., Mark S. Gold, Norman S. Miller, and A. Carter Pottash. "Sexual Dysfunction in Abusers of Cocaine and Alcohol." *Resident and Staff Physician* (September 1988):57–62.

Cocores, James A., Mark S. Gold, Robert K. Davies and Peter S. Mueller. "Cocaine Abuse and Adult Attention Deficit Disorder." *The Journal of Clinical Psychiatry* 48:9 (September 1987):376–377.

Cohen, Sidney. "Marijuana" (Chapter 11), *Annual Review of Psychiatry*, Volume 5 (1986). Washington, D.C.: American Psychiatric Press. 200–211.

Cook, Christopher C. H. "The Minnesota Model in the Management of Drug and Alcohol Dependency: Miracle, Method or Myth? Part I. The Philosophy and the Programme." *British Journal of Addiction* 83 (1988):625–634.

Corty, Eric, Charles P. O'Brien and Stephan Mann. "Reactivity to

Alcohol Stimuli in Alcoholics: Is There a Role for Temptation?" *Drug and Alcohol Dependence* 21 (1988):29–36.

Dogoloff, Lee I. "What's Wrong With Marijuana?" *Fair Oaks Hospital Psychiatry Letter* 5:9 (September 1987):44–49.

Duckert, Fanny and Jon Johnsen. "Behavioral Use of Disulfiram in the Treatment of Problem Drinking." *The International Journal of the Addictions* 22:5 (1987):445–454.

Edwards, Griffith, David Brown, Anni Duckitt et al. "Outcome of Alcoholism: The Structure of Patient Attributions as to What Causes Change." *British Journal of Addiction* 82 (1987):533–545.

Emrick, Chad D. "Alcoholics Anonymous: Affiliation Processes and Effectiveness as Treatment." *Alcoholism: Clinical and Experimental Research* 11:5 (September/October 1987):416–423.

Extein, I. L., and Mark S. Gold. "The Treatment of Cocaine Addicts: Bromocriptine or Desipramine." *Psychiatric Annals* 18:9 (September 1988):535–537.

Filstead, William J. "Monitoring the Process of Recovery Using Electronic Pagers as a Treatment Intervention." *Recent Developments in Alcoholism* (1988):181–191.

Foon, Anne E. "The Effectiveness of Drinking-Driving Treatment Programs: A Critical Review." *The International Journal of the Addictions* 23:2 (1988):151–174.

Foote, Andrea and John C. Erfurt. "Post Treatment Follow-up, Aftercare and Worksite Reentry of the Recovering Alcoholic Employee." *Recent Developments in Alcoholism* (1988):193–204.

Francis, Richard, Valery Yandow and George Alexopoulos. "Alcoholism: The Widening Scope." *Fair Oaks Hospital Psychiatry Letter* 2:3, (March 1984):1–4.

Gawin, Frank H., and Herbert D. Kleber. "Evolving Conceptualizations of Cocaine Dependence." *The Yale Journal of Biology and Medicine* 61 (1988):123–126.

Gelman, David, Lisa Drew, Mary Hager et al. "Roots of Addiction." *Newsweek* (February 20, 1989):52–57.

Giangrego, Elizabeth. "Chemical Dependency: the Road to Recovery." *JADA* 115 (July 1987):17–27.

Gilbert, Francis S. "The Effect of Type of Aftercare Follow-Up on Treatment Outcome Among Alcoholics." *Journal of Studies on Alcohol* 49:2 (1988):149–159.

Gitlow, Stanley E. "The Pharmacological Approach to Alcoholism."
Maryland State Medical Journal 19 (April 1970):93–96.

Glatt, M. M. (Letter) *British Journal of Hospital Medicine* (June 1987):
555–556.

Gold, Mark S. "Alcoholism: Disease and Denial." *Alcoholism and Addiction* (July/August 1988):15.

Gold, Mark S. and Karl Verebey. "From Coca Leaves to Crack: The Effects of Dose and Routes of Administration in Abuse Liability." *Psychiatric Annals* 18:9 (September 1988):513–520.

Gold, Mark S., and Herb Roehrich. "800-COCAINE: 1988." *The Yale Journal of Biology and Medicine* (1988).

Gold, Mark S., and Herb Roehrich. "Emergency Presentations of Crack Abuse." *Emergency Medical Services* 17:8 (September 1988):41–44.

Goodwin, Donald W. "Alcoholism and Genetics: The Sins of the Fathers." *Archives of General Psychiatry* 42 (February 1985):171–174.

Harrison, Patricia Ann, and Carol A Belille. "Women in Treatment: Beyond the Stereotype." *Journal of Studies on Alcohol* 48:6 (1987): 574–578.

Haver, B. "Female Alcoholics: III. Patterns of Consumption 3–10 Years After Treatment." *Acta Psychiatr. Scand.* 75 (1987):397–404.

Hitri, Ana., Richard Suddath, Diane Venable, and Richard J. Wyatt. "Loss of Dopamine Reutake Sites Following Cocaine." Presented at the American Psychiatric Association Meeting, San Francisco, (1989).

Hoard, Pamela S. "Premenstrual Syndrome Can Trigger Relaspe." *Alcoholism and Addiction* (July/August 1988):41.

Holden, Constance. "Is Alcoholism a Disease?" *News and Comment* (December 18, 1987):1647.

Horwitz, Ralph I., Sarah M. Horwitz, Catherine M. Viscoli, Louis D. Gottlieb and Mark L. Kraus. "Second Thoughts: Craving and the Social Context: A New Interaction Model for Enhancing Recovery From Alcoholism." *Journal of Chronic Diseases* 40:12 (1987):1135–1140.

Hoyumpa, Anastacio M.: "Alcohol Interactions with Benzodiazepines and Cocaine," in *Advances in Alcohol and Substance Abuse* Vol. 3, No. 4, Summer 1984. Haworth Press, Inc.

Jaffee, Jerome H. "Opiods" (Chapter 8) *Annual Review of Psychiatry,*

Volume 5 (1986). Washington, D.C.: American Psychiatric Press. 137–159.

Ketcham, Katherine; Mueller, L. Ann: *Eating Right to Live Sober*. Signet (NAL Penguin), New York, 1983.

King, Paul. "Heavy Metal Music and Drug Abuse in Adolescents." *Post Graduate Medicine* 83:5 (April 1988):295–304.

Kleber, Herbert D. "Introduction: Cocaine Abuse: Historical, Epidemiological and Psychological Perspectives." *Journal of Clinical Psychiatry* 49:2 (February 1988):3–5.

Kleber, Herbert D. "Treatment of Narcotic Addicts." *Psychiatric Medicine* (1987):389–418.

Kleber, Herbert D., and Frank H. Gawin. "Cocaine" (Chapter 9) *Annual Review of Psychiatry*, Volume 5 (1986). Washington, D.C.: American Psychiatric Press. 160–185.

Knouse, V. H., and H. G. Schneider. "Recovering Alcoholics: Personality and Aftercare Factors." *Psychological Reports* 61 (1987):595–601.

Kosten, Thomas R., Behnaz Jalali, John H. Steidl and Herbert D. Kleber. "Relationship of Marital Structure and Interactions to Opiate Abuse Relapse." *American Journal of Drug and Alcohol Abuse* 13:4 (1987):387–399.

Kritsberg, Wayne. *The Adult Children of Alcoholics Syndrome: A Step-by-Step Guide to Discovery and Recovery*. Bantam Books, New York, 1988.

Kunin, Richard A: *Mega-Nutrition*. Signet (NAL Penguin), New York, 1981.

LaJeunesse, Charles A. and Richard W. Thoreson. "Generalizing a Predictor of Male Alcoholic Treatment Outcomes." *The International Journal of the Addictions* 23:2 (1988):183–205.

Lewis, Alan: *Combined Monoamine Deficits in Cocaine Abuse: Strategic Partitioning of Neurotransmitter Precursors*. Astra Research Corporation, Berkeley, California, 1989.

Living Sober. Alcoholics Anonymous World Services, Inc., New York, 1975.

Macdonald, J. Grant. "Predictors of Treatment Outcome for Alcoholic Women." *The International Journal of the Addictions* 22:3 (1987):235–248.

Madara, Edward J., and Abigail Meese. *The Self-Help Sourcebook:*

Finding and Forming Mutual Aid Self-Help Groups (second edition). Denville, N.J.: Self-Help Clearinghouse, Saint Clares–Riverside Medical Center, 1988.

Maisto, Stephen A., Timothy J. O'Farrell, Gerard J. Connors, James R. McKay and Margorie Pelcovits. "Alcoholics' Attributions of Factors Affecting Their Relapse to Drinking and Reasons For Terminating Relapse Episodes." *Addictive Behaviors* 13:1 (1988):79–82.

Marjot, D. H. (letter). *British Journal of Hospital Medicine* (June 1987): 556.

Milam, James R.; Ketcham, Katherine: *Under the Influence.* Bantam, New York, 1983.

Milkman, Harvey B., and Howard J. Shaffer (Editors). *The Addictions: Multidisciplinary Perspectives and Treatments* Massachusetts/Toronto: Lexington Books.

Miller, William R., A. Lane Leckman, and Martha Tinkcom (letter). *Journal of the American Medical Association* 257:23 (June 19, 1987): 3228–3229.

Millman, Robert B. "Afterword." *Annual Review of Psychiatry*, Volume 5 (1986). Washington, D.C.: American Psychiatric Press. 226–227.

Millman, Robert B. "Drug Abuse and Drug Dependence." (Section II) *Annual Review of Psychiatry*, Volume 5 (1986). Washington, D.C.: American Psychiatric Press. 121–135.

Moyer, Mary A. "Stepping Beyond Survival to Recovery." *Alcoholism and Addiction* (July/August 1988):46–47.

Myers, Judy; Mellin, Maribeth: *Staying Sober.* Congden & Weed, 1987.

Neidigh, Larry W., Ellis L. Gesten and Saul Shiffman. "Coping with the Temptation to Drink." *Addictive Behavior* 13:1 (1988):1–9.

Niaura, Raymond S., Damaris J. Rohsenow, Jody A. Binkoff et al. "Relevance of Cue Reactivity to Understanding Alcohol and Smoking Relapse." *Journal of Abnormal Psychology* 97:2 (1988):133–152.

Ogborne, Alan C. "A Note on the Characteristics of Alcohol Abusers With Controlled Drinking Aspirations." *Drug and Alcohol Dependence* 19 (1987):159–164.

Öjehagen, Agneta, Anne Skjaerris and Mats Berglund. "Prediction of Posttreatment Drinking Outcome in a 2 year Out-Patient Alcoholic Treatment Program: A Follow-up Study." *Alcoholism: Clinical and Experimental Research* 12:1 (January/February 1988):46–51.

Plattner, Andy, and Gorden Witkin. "Drugs on Main Street: The Enemy up Close." *U.S. News and World Report* (June 27, 1988):14–22.

Priestley, Joan C: *Your Life-Enhancing Diet.* Joan C. Priestley, M.D., Santa Monica, California, 1989.

Reiger, Gail. "Users, Like Me: Membership in the Church of Drugs." *Harper's Magazine* (May 1989):51–54.

Reuler, James B., et al: "Wernicke's encephalopathy," in *New England Journal of Medicine* Vol. 312, No. 16, April 18, 1985.

Robertson, Nan. "The Changing World of Alcoholics Anonymous." *New York Times Magazine* (1988).

Roelofs, Sarah M., and Gerard M. Dikkenberg. "Hyperventilation and Anxiety: Alcohol Withdrawal Symptoms Decreasing With Prolonged Abstinence." *Alcohol* 4 (1987):215–220.

Rounsaville, Bruce J., Thomas R. Kosten, and Herbert D. Kleber. "The Antecedents and Benefits of Achieving Abstinence in Opioid Addicts: A 2.5 Year Follow-up Study." *American Journal of Drug and Alcohol Abuse* 13:3 (1987):213–229.

Roy-Byrne, Peter P.; Uhde, Thomas W: "Exogenous factors in panic disorder: Clinical and research implications," in *Journal of Clinical Psychiatry* Vol. 49, No. 2, February, 1988.

Rud, R.C., and K. Magee. "Prevention of Relapse With Treatment of Depression in Alcoholic Patients: An Exploratory Study." *Alberta Association of Registered Nurses Newsletter* 43:4 (April 1987):4–5.

Ruzek, Joe. "Identifying and Helping." *Occupational Health* (April 1987):120–122.

Scott, Neil. "Attraction Vs. Promotion: Stop Sending People to AA." *Alcoholism and Addiction* (July/August 1988):5.

Shaffer, Howard J. "Conceptual Crises and the Addictions: A Philosophy of Science Perspective." *Journal of Substance Abuse Treatment* 3 (1986):285–296.

Shaffer, Howard J. "The Epistemology of 'Addictive Disease': The Lincoln-Douglas Debate." *Journal of Substance Abuse Treatment* 4 (1987):103–113.

Sheeren, Mary. "The Relationship Between Relapse and Involvement in Alcoholics Anonymous." *Journal of Studies on Alcohol* 49:1 (April 1987):104–106.

Skutle, Arvid and Geir Berg. "Training in Controlled Drinking for

Early-Stage Problem Drinkers." *British Journal of Addiction* 82 (1987): 493–501.

Smith, David E. "Decreasing Drug Hunger." *Professional Counselor* (November–December 1988).

Steinberg, John. "The Role of AA in Treatment and Recovery of Impaired Professionals." *MMJ* 36:3 (March 1987):241–244.

Tennant, Forest. "Clinical Diagnosis and Treatment of Post Drug Impairment Syndrome." *Psychiatry Letter*, Fair Oaks Hospital, Summit N.J. 47–51.

Thurstin, Adrian H., and Anthony M. Alfano. "The Association of Alcoholic Subtype With Treatment Outcome: An 18 Month Follow-Up." *The International Journal of the Addictions* 23:3 (1988):321–330.

Trachtenberg, Michael C., and Kenneth Blum. "Improvement of Cocaine-Induced Neuromodulator Deficits by the Neuronutrient Tropamine." *Journal of Psychoactive Drugs* 20:3 (July–September 1988):315–331.

Ward, Janice L., and Howard J. Shaffer. "Narcotic and Other Drug Use: A Spectrum." *Journal of Substance Abuse Treatment* 3 (1986):297–299.

Watson, Charles G. "Recidivism in 'Controlled Drinker' Alcoholics: A Longitudinal Study." *Journal of Clinical Psychology* 43:3 (May 1987):404–412.

Wegscheider, Don. *If Only My Family Understood Me . . .* , Minneapolis, CompCare Publishers, 1979.

Winstanley, George. "Recovery Programmes." *Occupational Health* (April 1987):112–114.

Woody, George E., A. Thomas McLellan, Lester Luborsky and Charles P. O'Brien. "Twelve Month Follow-up of Psychotherapy for Opiate Dependence." *American Journal of Psychiatry* 144:5 (May 1987):590–596.

INDEX

seeking of, 17–18
support groups, 43–45
surgery, pain relievers for, 94–95

teenagers:
  as COAs, 168
  marijuana use among, 65
  special problems among, 84–85
Tennant, Forrest, 85
terminal uniqueness, overcoming of, 33–35
trazodone, 61, 63
treatment programs, 9–10
  AA orientation of, 28, 53–55
  and absence of happy endings, 46–47
  acknowledging warped relationships and, 40
  aftercare in, 29, 51–53
  aims of, 23–24
  certified alcoholism counselors in, 28
  for codependency, 155–56
  cost of, 27
  crisis intervention in, 27
  drug screening in, 28–29
  duration of, 48
  expressing real feelings in, 35–37
  finding your place after, see rehabilitation, life after forced, 25
  getting good counseling in, 31–32
  highs from, 69–70
  hot seat in, 49–51
  inpatient vs. outpatient, 25–29
  licensed therapists in, 28
  mapping out new relationships in, 41
  medical and psychiatric care in, 27–28
  overcoming denial in, 30–31
  overcoming terminal uniqueness in, 33–35
  principles of, 23
  protective environment provided by, 19
  providing moment-to-moment answers in, 37–40
  psychological testing in, 27
  restoring support in, 42–43

selection of, 24–25
social evaluation in, 28
support groups in, 43–45
surviving change in, 41–42
understanding paradox in, 29
using group therapy in, 32–33
what to expect in, 23–55
as work, 55
tryptophan, 61, 107
Twelve Step Program, 9, 18, 52–53
Tylenol, 93
tyrosine, 61, 106–7

underweight, 98

Valium, 67, 94
vegetables, 104
vitamin supplements, 61, 106

warm-up exercises, 108
Wegscheider, Don, 144–45
willpower, 8, 148–49
withdrawal, 60–69
  from alcohol, 62–63
  antidepressants for symptoms of, 59, 61, 63, 69
  from cocaine, 63–65
  from marijuana, 65–66
  from narcotics, 66–67
  from prescription medications, 67–68
  from psychedelic drugs, 68–69
women:
  low self-esteem in, 82–83
  PMS in, 82–83
  risks of alcohol during pregnancy in, 90–91
  sexual abuse of, 82–84
  sexual problems in, 174–75, 178–179
  special problems among, 82–84
work:
  being asked to name chemically dependent employees at, 199–200
  efforts to exert control at, 209–10
  after rehab, 198–200
  relapses caused by, 126
  tuning out noise about, 205

ABOUT THE AUTHOR

JAMES A. COCORES, M.D., is medical director of the Outpatient Recovery Centers of Fair Oaks Hospital. As one of the largest providers of outpatient treatment for chemical dependency in the United States, Fair Oaks Hospital operates six outpatient facilities, all directed by Dr. Cocores. A pioneer in the outpatient treatment movement during the last decade, Dr. Cocores is renowned for his innovative research and charismatic teaching. He has pioneered new treatments for codependency, cocaine dependency, and pathological gambling. He has frequently appeared on national television and radio programs including ABC's *Eyewitness News*, *Good Morning America*, and *CBS This Morning*. He is also frequently interviewed in national media such as *USA Today*, *The New York Times*, *The Washington Post*, and *The Wall Street Journal*. Dr. Cocores lectures extensively to concerned family members and has published more than forty-five scientific articles and professional studies in the areas of drug abuse, codependency, recovery, and addiction.